V.I.P.

Very Interesting Perspectives...*

My 68+ Years on Planet Earth...
By Phil Schaefer

Table of Contents

THE ONLY WAY TO START IS TO START.

The attempt is often painful, but *The Attempt* is all we have. Anonymous and so very true.

Very Interesting Perspectives includes my Autobiography. *A Real Piece of Work… My 68 years on planet earth,* as well as *Wait for it… Wait for it.* As Ruth's passing was a shock to us all, I found myself saying 'Said & Done' and making an effort to move forward with my personal journals, my life, and my 4th *TBC… To be continued* is indeed my effort to keep on keeping on. *Loose Ends & Screws* was added after three years of writing. It's life and pushes us forward, whether you are ready or not. All aboard then. Hold on tight.

I wrote my 1st journal to stay sane while Ruth was undergoing chemo for breast cancer, and it seemed to flow out of my head in just 2 months' time.

She told me she would not be reading it, and I told her that's fine, as I think she knew her ending would be different than mine. She was convinced her brain was broken after just one chemo treatment and lost all hope of ever being her old self ever again. Her decision to end it was hers to make. She could be very stubborn sometimes and had made up her mind. Sad but true, as we'd shared 22 years together in what I can only say was truly Heaven on Earth. We were blessed.

I hope you enjoy my recollections and honesty, and my humor as well, as I've always tried to include jocularity as often as I could. If you can't laugh at yourself, who can you laugh at?

No one ever said life would be easy, and as hard as some of my stories are, I've always tried to laugh through them with family and friends. I'm forever grateful to you all. *All y'all.*

Thank you so very much.

Moi. :)

"Our house… was a very, very, very fine house."

"A REAL PIECE OF WORK... MY 68 YEARS ON PLANET EARTH."

Chapter One: My Birth-Day

I'd been told that I might have some cognitive issues, so bear with me as I try to tell you my story. The audiologist at Costco told me that I might have a brain tumor. I had to actually try to make light of it as I turned to my wife and said, "Yay, a brain tumor! Lucky me." After further investigation via an MRI and more, it turned out that all I had was a hearing impairment. Thanks, Costco. They owe me $5000.00 for the expenses and torture they inflicted on me and my wife.

Anyway, I was born in NYC at 2:22 am with a birthmark on my left shoulder. Just so happens that my mom tested an old wives' tale that if a woman who is with child sees a mouse and touches herself, the child will be born with a mark. All I can say is I'm glad she didn't rub her nose.

What's also interesting is that some 33 years later, she shared that I was almost aborted, as my dad, a.k.a. my Papa, was not my biological father. News to me, as I told my mom that I'd expected some really bad news when she told me that we needed to talk. I thought she was going to tell me that she's dying or something worse. Long story short, she'd had a quick affair before her wedding day to my Papa, and he so loved her that it didn't matter to him. He knew I was not his, and she did not want to abort this one. Mind you, this is in 1953. Wow, I thought, as he never loved me any less than any of my siblings who came along later. Two brothers and a sister later, they never let on. He loved her and us very much, and it was only while on vacation that my brother and sister asked if she had any secrets she wanted to share. They were floored and almost sorry they'd asked. The truth was out, and my mom then just had to share it with me. I tell you this because I really shouldn't be here, and feel blessed at my age to have lived a wonderful life. It hasn't been an easy life, but it's important to know this before going any further.

Here goes:

My father's name was Fred, and my mom's Colette. They fled Europe because he was Jewish, and she, being French, was living in Paris, where it simply was no longer a safe place to be. She went to Quebec, Canada, and he to New York to enlist in the Army. He needed to go back. He was fluent in German, so they made him a spy, and for two years, he somehow survived the unimaginable.

Chapter Two: Psych-Test

"You're emotionally un-integrated," my psychiatrist told me. My response was, "Well, aren't we all?" and I walked away. I was 23 when our Papa died in a car crash on March 5th, 1977. My sister's best friend Judy came into my room and woke me with the news. Being the older brother, I had to then share it with my mom and sister. Their reaction was exactly what I'd expected. Worst news ever!! I decided to go to my employer at the Concord Hotel, where I'd been working as a Bellhop, to tell them I wasn't going to be coming back.

The kicker is that my dad's business was struggling, and I was giving my mom everything I was making from tips to keep our family going. Every morning, I'd confirm that there was something there for her. It kept us fed, and I was glad to do it. Kept the lights on too. Over the many years of visiting her, she'd always throw me a few hundred dollars to cover my expenses. We both knew that life was expensive and it was always appreciated. I still have the last $100 she gave me in my wallet for good luck. The shared experiences of surviving are layered in the sharing of what we had at the time. Always appreciated and always a bit emotional as well.

My upset with my Papa the night before his death, because I'd come to the conclusion that the only way this situation at home was going to change was, in fact, with his dying. A death wish of sorts, as our family was barely holding on at that point. It still hurts to recall. It's important, though, to hear my story, as it's ours as well.

I must say that he did pay me the ultimate compliment before his death, and that was that he was proud of me. He never said this to my brothers or sister, and ultimately, it added to my shame and grief years later. Decades later.

I couldn't share any of this until I had a breakdown and thanks to my brother, Sandy went to spend an extended stay at Arden Hill Mental Health Dept where I shared my story avoiding the conclusion my therapist finally told me at the end of my 30 days "You didn't kill your father" she blurted out exposing my raw nerve to the rest of our little group. I later wrote this song to a Bob Dylan tune changing the words to "Arden Hill, Arden Hill … Everybody here seems over-the-hill … All you got to do is take a pill … then everything's fine at Arden Hill … Know what brought me to Arden

Hill … couldn't do nothing against my will … So I shed a tear and I spilled the beans… Went from Superman to Mr. Clean… So I'll be leaving Arden Hill, not quite sure if I'm over that hill … Don't know where to get that pill … Want to go back to Arden Hill." I shared it with everyone before leaving, and they all loved it.

Back into the world I went, working with family in the Auction Business. *World Wide Imports* was our company name, and we did auctions at some of the Hotels in and around *The Catskills* of New York. It was brutal.

On our day off, we needed to drive two hours to NYC to replenish our inventory of Brass, Crystal, and Porcelain items, along with some oriental handmade screens. Once home, we had to unbox, price, and re-box into some crates we'd made for safe transport to the next auction. Not counting the drive to and from, the unloading and set up, the teardown and the occasional visit to the hotel game room, an auction could last about two hours. The auction itself usually lasted only an hour. "Here Kutuchu-Go!" meant we're off to Kutcher's Hotel again, and it became our daily mantra, meaning "We're off to yet another auction." They seemed endless and exhausting.

My brother was very good at what he did and developed a unique style of winning over the audience during each and every show. He could get folks crying with laughter when he'd describe how the delicate hand painting was done with the wings of Tit-sie flies. Very large-breasted flies that were easy to spot thanks to the cute little white halter tops and, of course, easy to catch because of the large Tit-sies. Hysterical, I laughed almost every time I heard it, seeing the audience crack up. He had them in the palm of his hand as the bid would then go higher and higher. It was a hoot as he knew exactly what he was doing.

My youngest brother Marc was even called into the mix and, at 14, was driving our van into NYC without a license, because we needed him to. Once when he stopped to pay a toll, the woman taking his payment looked at him and knew that there was no way he was old enough to be driving. She let him pass because, well, that's NY for ya. Over time, he also became the youngest auctioneer ever. He enjoyed it and the money too. It was all hands-on deck in those days, and if Papa were alive, he would have told his youngest son that he was proud of him as well. We all were. We should have told him so, but never did.

I was hanging in there, thanks to the occasional joint or two as it was my way of coping with exhaustion, depression, and loneliness as well. I quit the auction business when a roommate of a girlfriend of mine shared that a new solar energy start-up was something I should try to get into. Bio-Energy was their name, and I was hired, earning about $150 a week because they simply couldn't afford more. I was on board with the potential of earning more later. Over time, I transitioned from working with one other person in their Shop as a two-person team to becoming the Factory Manager of approximately two dozen workers.

I loved it, as we all enjoyed what we were doing and believed in the dream. Then, I got involved in a relationship with one of the office secretaries, and while it lasted, it was good. Until it wasn't ultimately leading to me resigning. My bad, as she was sweet but had marriage on her agenda. I wasn't ready and, in hindsight, made the right decision. Sorry Thelma.

At times, it felt like every day was a Psych test: Pass or fail? Some days I'd pass and other days not so much. Is what it is.

One day at a time … "Here Kutuchu-Go."

Chapter Three: Where Do I Begin?

My parents met in NYC at an Arthur Murray Dance Studio, where he asked her to dance. They were both exceptional dancers, and La Force del Destino became their song. Soon after, they fell in love and married on St Patrick's Day in 1953.

My father's mom was the only witness, and what sounded like her sobbing was instead her trying her best to hold back the laughter of pure joy. Tzilie was her name, and all three of them ended up laughing at the pompous way of the person who married them that day.

I was, of course, there as well, and on October 20th was born. Fred was a bit surprised when he saw me and had to ask my mom if she'd seen me yet. It seemed that my head was a little misshapen, which I'm told isn't that unusual with newborn babies. I'm also told that I quickly grew into being a beautiful baby boy. A couple of years later came my brother and I suggested that they take him back, as I knew things were about to change and I wasn't ready for any of it. Then, my sister came and when I was ten my second brother arrived as well. We were a family. Phil, Sandy, Nicole, and Marc. My mom gave us all French names… Philippe Jean, Alexandre Paul, Nicole Yvette, and Marc with a "c" Marc Gerard. All of us Schaefers.

In German, the name Schaefer means Shepherd. My mom's maiden name was Bergé, which also translates to means the same. The same meaning… They were the shepherds, and we were their sheep. We lived in NYC and moved into an apartment not far from Gracie Mansion, located at 1700 York Ave. NY Apartment 8J. The eighth floor meant that I could throw my plastic soldiers with parachutes made from paper napkins and watch them land on the Building's Entrance canopy. It was so much fun to watch.

I wonder if they're still there.

I remember going to the Park and playing, feeling safe and loved. Until my bike was stolen one day, and I realized that there was an evil side to living in the Big City. I also had some great babysitters, but no one compared to my Grandma. She was the personification of love… A beautiful person.

A first grandchild is a big deal, and I was cherished in her company. She always had some candy for me in her purse or, at the very least, some

Smith Brothers Cough Drops, but she also had a chocolate bar that I simply couldn't have. Why, I thought?

Because it was X-Lax and I wanted some. It was the only "no."

I have ever heard her say … "No."

My Papa played piano, so when I was about five or six, she actually bought me a miniature piano. I didn't understand how it made music, so I took it apart and destroyed her wonderful gift. I was too young, and even though it must have broken her heart, she never said a word about it.

Cut from the same tree, Papa once gave my brother and me $5.00 so we could buy some ice cream from a Mr. Softy's. Assuming that it was ours to spend, he was a bit shocked when, upon our return, he asked for his change, and I had to tell him that we'd spent it all. Back then, that was a lot of ice cream. Our 1st lesson with money was that day.

Money was always an issue for my dad, and when he met my mom, I think she tried to help him with suggestions. They started a company called Aladdin's and designed and manufactured a miniature cigarette lighter in Silver & Gold, and some with precious stones.

Imagine their delight when Betty Davis used their lighter to light her cigarette in a movie titled All About Eve. Wow, right?

I actually have one that my mom gave me, and it's beautifully made. Very special indeed. Then somehow the Japanese decided to create a knock-off, which put them out of business. They tried to introduce a tiny pistol that sprayed perfume; however, there were too many production issues to make it work. My dad tried to become a stockbroker/business middleman.

His business ventures finally did pay off one day with an oil deal he helped broker. He made at least half a million dollars, maybe more. We never knew the exact amount. He bought himself his dream car, a Jaguar sedan. My Mom got her Mustang. My brother and I got Mgs. It was grand. Until his partner stole almost everything, it was nice while it lasted, and at least he got to taste the good life, and for that I'm glad.

Chapter Four: We're Moving

My parents were clever for the time and decided that we needed more room. They got permission from the landlord to rent the adjacent apartment and created an opening to make it one larger unit. It also made it more expensive and one day, all of our stuff was outside on the sidewalk. As kids, we never saw it and only heard about it years later. Can you imagine?

My dad went into emergency mode and arranged to purchase a 2-bedroom Bungalow on 5 acres of land from a relative who wanted out. Ant Julia was her name, and so Upstate NY here we come... Sullivan County Catskills.

"Going up to the country." And it was 1963, the same year

J.F. Kennedy was shot in Dallas, became my last memory of being in NYC I was in the locker room after a gym class at the Lycée Francais de NY when I heard the news. As a 10-year-old boy, I have to admit to shedding some tears that night for his loss. It was the 1st news event that hit me upside the head like it hit us all just that same way... We were all in shock because we'd lost someone special on that day of 11/22/63, and the 60s were here.

Up Fish Hatchery Rd. in Summitville, NY, to the very top we drove. The last part of the road was about an eighth of a mile and was rough, but it was ours, so it was cool. The house was a two-bedroom and there were six of us. My brother and I got the smaller bedroom and were at home in our new Bunk bed. My sister got the sofa in the living room while my youngest brother still a baby, slept in my parents' room.

Our mom made it a home from day one as we all made the best of it. We explored a detached garage and found a hammock, which we quickly realized fit perfectly between two trees right in front of our new little house. Imagine me, my brother, and my sister in this hammock for the very first time. Sharing a vivid imagination, we got this new imaginary boat rocking & rolling down the rapids. Each one of us falling out due to the extreme swinging we were able to achieve... So much fun.

We loved our new home and began to venture out into the woods, marveling at Mother Nature. Birds, deer, raccoons, wild turkeys, and more. We even found a Bungalow colony about a mile away. Once, when there was no one there, the three of us went to the center of the field separating the dozen or more bungalows. My brother and I suddenly heard what sounded like an animal's growl. When we looked up the hill we soon realized that a bear had spotted us and wasn't pleased with our being there and charged towards us. We grabbed my sister's hands and started to run, making it back home safely with her feet never touching the ground. That was close, we all agreed. Too close for comfort and an important lesson we needed to learn.

Further exploring our garage, my brother and I found two hatchets along with a 3-foot-long 4" by 4" wood block. We instantly became Indian Braves swinging our hatchets one at a time into the vertical post, until I missed. My hatchet came down on my knee, making a 2-inch cut… Probably should have gotten stitches, but instead, we treated my wound ourselves, never speaking a word of it to my parents. Figured we'd keep this one to ourselves.

Chapter Five: Winter!

Our new floor plan included a screened-in front porch. It was a great space that let the outside in. My brother and I loved sleeping out there as it was like camping, but better. As fall turned to winter, we'd challenge ourselves to sleeping on the porch. As it got colder and we could see our breath, our mom gave us extra blankets and even an electric blanket to keep us from freezing to death and as it went below 32°F. It was time to come inside, she told us… We agreed.

Keeping warm in a house designed for the summer was interesting as we all became expert fire makers in a pot-bellied stove. Originally, gathering wood and buying coal became our survival mode, as they were essential to the house. Early on, I became responsible for rebuilding the morning fire, and if I was lucky, there'd be a few orange coals left to rekindle a new fire. Fire good… Heat good.

Very good.

Winter also meant sledding, and man, did we have fun doing it. My dad, who was commuting daily to NYC for his work, asked me once if I could give him a ride on my sled so he could catch the bus, as driving that day was not an option due to snowfall. I said I'll give it a try, as some of the almost mile-long hill was pretty steep and our speed could become a concern. He was ready and positioned himself on the back of my sled with his attaché case separating us. Off we went, down one hill and then another. It was a wild ride, but we made it. He got up, thanked me and kissed me goodbye. We were an affectionate family hugging and kissing quite often.

One winter, it snowed about a foot in the early afternoon. My mom knew that my dad would be coming home later and would not make up our road unless it was cleared. On her own, she swept and shoveled our long driveway. It took her hours. He made it home that night as she taught us that we always make a Herculean Effort for the ones we love… Always.

My mom, being French, knew how to cook and could turn an ordinary Chicken into a gourmet meal. She could also make up a storm and get our little home smelling so delicious. As kids, we'd hover around her hoping for a taste of raw dough as she made her croissants. Her Crepes were divine with just a small sprinkle of sugar. She also used to stuff them with Chicken

Livers & Onions dipped in egg as it was one of Papa's favorite dishes… Delicious.

On other occasions, she'd make him meals that were ones that he enjoyed, like Wiener Schnitzel and German Potato Salad, for example, and a Potato bread called Mandabutchen. To watch Papa eat this bread with more butter than any one person should ever consume was impressive. He was in heaven. I learned how to make it so we're all still able to enjoy it from time to time. It takes 3 hours but is so worth it. She's also used to make us what's called a Croque Monsieur, which was to die for. Yes, we grew up eating well, and I thought everybody did. I was wrong.

In the public school's cafeteria, I remember the two Percell brothers creating a mashed potato sandwich to satisfy their hunger… "Reality, what a concept." Robin Williams … I learned that there were those who had and those who did not. I felt blessed as I was among those who had.

Chapter Six: Papa Wants To Build

My dad, being from Europe, told us Vienna, I'm not sure. He escaped to the US and joined the Army in the hope of rescuing his family from certain death. He managed to save his mother & her mother, Clair, along with a few others. Very few others. When he returned after being discharged, his nerves were understandably shot to the point where he grew a beard because he couldn't shave. He'd shake terribly. It looked good, and he looked a bit like an early beatnik musician. Very hip. We found out later that he'd been a spy for the US because he spoke German. Can you imagine the guts it must have taken during his couple of years of service? He told us a story of his cover being blown once, and as the German officer tried to shoot him with his Luger pistol, it jammed, giving my dad the chance to shoot and kill him so as to get away. Truly unbelievable that he survived.

He had an appreciation of European architecture and design, so he knew what our little bungalow could eventually become. We never really shared his vision until later. As a DIY project, it was only in his head as he directed the work to begin. We all unknowingly volunteered to be his work crew, and every weekend he'd wake us bright and early to a Viennese March playing on his record player. He loved waking us with music blaring. Okay, we get it as we'd find out what he had in mind for the day. On The Keeve eve, he'd say, as if it meant something.

Our 1st project was to build a Terrace in front of our beloved porch. First, we had to dig and pour a foundation. Mixing cement in a mixer he bought required an exact combination of sand, cement, and water. We had to pour it in one day so as not to have any cold seams. That made for one extremely long day, with lights on at night and mom serving us sandwiches to keep us going. After that, it was time to lay blocks. I got pretty good at cutting 8-inch cement blocks as we built row upon row to the desired height of about 8 feet. We did it.

Once it was done, we ordered a load of dirt to be dumped into the hole the blocks created. The dump truck came and bumped our new terrace by accident, and a few days later, it all came crashing down as it collapsed. We should have used 12-inch cinder blocks and not 8-inch ones was our conclusion. It was time for my mom to jump in and, with my brother's help, clean it up and prepare the area for a do-over… The lesson was that of perseverance.

I must add that while we were digging the trenches for the foundation to be poured, we encountered a boulder about 30 inches in diameter. We knew eventually it was going to have to come out, but we weren't ready to deal with it just yet. When it became necessary to remove, we were ready with a crowbar and pickaxe to get it done. It, however, wasn't going anywhere.

My dad's mom was visiting that weekend and appreciated the situation. Without saying anything to any of us, she stepped into the trench and bent over the boulder and embraced it with both arms wrapped around it, and in one motion, she pivoted using her legs and lifted it two feet up and out. It was amazing and was her awesome contribution to our day's work. Her body was perfectly sized and shaped for this one task. "Pivot!" "Pivot!"

After the terrace, the bigger picture of a Swiss Chalet was slowly but surely was to be built around the original existing bungalow. It took us years, but eventually came to be. It was his dream come true, and we remain in awe to this day, even though we no longer have the house in our possession. It remains in our minds as a cherished childhood experience. The house we'd built with him taught us more than I can say, my brother and I. We built it.

Unfortunately, he didn't live to see it finished. We had to do that without him. His spirit was there, and we all continued to talk about it and him to this day, years later. He's still with us. "Oh my Papa, to me he was so wonderful … Oh my Papa, to me he was so good." was a song that he taught us to appreciate subconsciously. He occasionally would also sing "If I Were a Rich Man… Bidie-Bidie-Bidie-Bidie-Bidie-Bum… All day long I'd Bidie-Bidie-Bum IF I were a wealthy man." He had a quirky sense of humor and a unique smile as well. We never heard him laugh out loud, but he loved hearing us laugh. He also loved telling us the occasional dirty joke to see our reactions. Mum would just shake her head.

He also loved his cigarettes and always smelled of smoke. Every New Year's Eve, he actually said that we could smoke a cigarette if we wanted. Of course, we did. None of us ended up liking it very much and never smoked later in life… At least not cigarettes.

Chapter Seven: School Days

In NYC, I'd been going to a French private school. When it was time for school in Upstate NY, my parents decided to try homeschooling. Awesome while it lasted, but it didn't. In private school, we wore a suit & tie, so on our 1st day of Public school, I wore the same. Big mistake, as all the kids that day had themselves a good old laugh. "Why are you all wearing a suit and tie?" they asked. It was 6th grade, and Mrs. Bennet was my teacher back then. A little different than Private school. I liked it, and the girls in my class were pretty too, which helped.

School was never our strong point. Once, my brother and I hid our Report Cards from our parents for almost two months, as they were issued every 10 weeks. I kept mine neatly folded in a book while my brother kept his in his pocket for eight weeks! When we finally shared them, our parents knew something wasn't right. My dad actually told us to consider learning a trade. It scared the begenas out of us, and we tried a little harder. Not a lot harder, mind you, just a little harder.

Some of our schooling continued at home with Papa's queries at the dinner table, asking us if we knew the capitals of European countries or current events. His nightly ritual of watching the news was forced upon us in black and white, featuring Chet Huntley and David Brinkley. Vietnam involvement continued ad-infinitum over the years with daily death tolls becoming more & more meaningless, until I realized in 12th grade that being 18 in 1972 meant that I could be drafted. Holly Shit! What if I were drafted? Would I be able to get out of it? I'll never know, as my number came up very high, so it never happened.

Another little something I missed back in 1969 was Woodstock. I was 16 and could drive, but my parents said no. But, but, but was to no avail, and as close as we were to where the festival actually took place in Bethel, NY, I'd be forced to watch it unfold on the nightly news. "The NY State Thruway is closed, man," but for me, it was not meant to be. Go to the Museum built on this site if ever you can to experience 1st hand what it must have been like, as half a million people showed up for 3 Days of Fun and Music on Yasgur's Farm. They warned everyone not to take the brown acid/LSD that was being offered, as it wasn't a good trip, they claimed.

A couple of years later, I did get to see the movie and remember paying $5.00 to get in. OMG, I thought, as this just won't be a price folks would ever be willing to pay to see any movie in the future. It was worth the price of admission, and I felt like I was there for a few precious hours. All the musicians were exceptional, especially Crosby, Stills, Nash & Young, who were playing together for the first time. "You, who are on the road… Must have a code… that you can live by."

My eyes and ears were opened to music and concert-going.

Emerson, Lake & Palmer was my first concert, followed by James

Taylor and I even got to see Richie Havens at The Joyous Lake in the actual town of Woodstock, about an hour away. I got within three feet of the man as he played Freedom and it was simply amazing. Freakin' amazing!!

I also explored the area and found the best Chinese restaurant ever in the adjacent town of Bearsville called The Little Bear. They offered up some green, peanut-flavored noodles that were beyond compare. I try to get back there every now and again just for those noodles. My sister knows this all too well.

My point being that my schooling was now out of the classroom.

Life experience was my new teacher, and because it was the late 60s and early 70s there were some drugs involved. Weed was always my favorite, but some occasional experimentation was expected of me in my circle of friends at the time. What can I say, except that if I could remember everything we did, then I wasn't really there. "I do not recall!" Shrooms were amazing, if I must admit. I was the one who could somehow drive. How we never got into an accident, I'll never know.

I graduated from Ellenville High School in 1972 and was off to College, as my Dad gave me the option of going to Israel, hoping that it would increase my appreciation of Judaism. It didn't, and in fact, I discovered Bethlehem and Christ. I actually stood where He was said to have delivered His Sermon on the Mount. Wow.

I never shared this with him, as it would have broken his heart.

I did meet my best friend Monte while at Tel-Aviv University.

More on him later. I graduated from High School, spent two years at Tel-Aviv University American Program, followed by one year at McGill University, thinking Architecture was to be my major, but after a year of prerequisite studies that included Calculus and Chemistry, I failed miserably. The next year, I entered my first year of a three-year program in Interior Design at the School of Art and Design at the Montreal Museum of Fine Arts. Yes, I loved it as I thought I'd finally found my niche, but it wasn't meant to be, as my Dad's business was failing. "Come home," he told me.

After four years of College, my father informed me that he could no longer afford my expenses. It was time for me to come home to help. I had to tell my girlfriend at the time that I would not be returning, and she was furious, as she'd already secured an apartment we'd agreed to share. My bad and my loss, as well as she was something else. Carol was her name, and to say it with a French accent used to take my breath away. Carol Garceau. She was a little older than I was and could give a really good blow-job. She introduced me to Vietnamese Cuisine in Montreal, which was fabulous. Something about those Spring Roles, if you know what I'm saying.

It was 1976-77, and it was strange to be back home, to say the least. It took me several attempts to find work that paid, but eventually I tried bell hopping at the Concord Hotel, a huge complex where, as one of a dozen or more Bellhops, I would move a thousand guests in and a thousand guests out on the same day. Brutal, but it paid. Every day, my pockets were stuffed with cash. $5's, $10's, and $20, and I gave almost all of it to my mom. It was our family's cash flow at the time. My dad's phone bills were astronomical as he tried his best to make something happen.

Times were changing, and things were not going well for him. He was stressed and worried as well. We all were.

One evening, when my dad was supposed to pick me up after work, he had forgotten. I had to call him to say I'm ready. More than ready. Why did I have to add another hour to my long day, I thought? I was pissed and when he finally got there, I told him I would drive, and so he switched seats. I drove my MG hard that night, working off my upset with him, and he was impressed with my driving. He told me when we got home.

The next day, he borrowed my car to go to the Post Office early that morning. The MGs were all we had left, and he wasn't a great driver, to put it mildly. His Jag was being repaired after a small collision that was his fault, and we couldn't afford the repair bill. He'd also totaled my Mom's Mustang. It was March, and the roads were icy. Very icy. He never made it home.

Chapter Eight: What Have I Done?

I'd had a premonition of sorts that my dad was about to die the night before his death. I remember standing at the top of the stairs and saying goodnight to him while sensing that this might be the last time I'd see him. I appreciated his facade as he walked away. Goodnight, then I said, aware of something being different but not sure what or why.

I personalized it, though, and had to hide it from the world when it happened. I'd wished him dead, or did I? No, I did not, I was told years later. "You did not kill your father," but to me, it sure felt like I had. Someone heard my thoughts that night before his death, thinking to myself that for things to change, he was going to have to die. We never knew what was so important to get in the mail that morning of March 5th, but on his return, he passed a car going into a curve and lost control. My MGB-GT did several 360s, hitting guard rails as it spun out, and the centrifugal force jettisoned him out the back hatch. Horrible. No seat belts back then. Even if the car had them, people didn't wear them. Why would you?

Anyway, with no Life Insurance to speak of, we were not in a good place. He may have had a $10,000 policy from his Army days, but that was it. What were the Schaefers going to do now to survive?

The answer came from my brother's involvement over the years with an Auction business selling gift items to hotel guests as a scheduled event for their entertainment. He knew the business, and we were all familiar. No other choice, as he partnered with someone he knew who would invest $10,000 to get it off and running.

The scheduling of as many as two and occasionally three auctions a day was too much and not worth the minimal financial return offered to me. But we kept the house going and food on the table, as the expression goes. I even found and bought a 1960 Corvette that my neighbor offered me for $ 4,000.00. How could I say anything but "I'll take it." Sweet.

Most impractical car ever, but it could do 50mph in 1st gear, and it was a 4-speed. My small-town mechanic serviced it for me once and informed me that there was but one bolt keeping that 283 small block engine in place. I eventually traded it for a van, and kick myself daily for parting with it. It was beautiful to look at, but it was not a daily driver. Oh well.

What's interesting was that now that our dad was no longer with us, his memory still was. Whenever we celebrated any holiday, we would always try our best to do it like he did. To sing a Hanukkah prayer with all the highs and lows was to bring him back to life for a moment. We tried to celebrate Passover Seders just like he used to do for us. It was great, but sad as well. He was no longer there.

Stories of what he said or did were remembered, including him asking us if we were "Telligent" or "Intelligent," making it sound like the latter was to be stupid. He'd also use foreign languages to label items. Cochravim and Shablon were two of his favorite. The 1st meaning stars in Hebrew, and the 2nd, I have no idea where it came from. "Pass me The Shablon," he repeated as we tried to figure out what the hell he was asking for… "The Shablon… The Shablon," he repeated, Not the Cochravim we'd ask? He smiled.

He also liked to use the word Schmuck a lot. It was his one and only curse word we ever heard him say… On occasion, he'd even call me a schmuck, and it hurt. He continued until one day at the dinner table, after he said it to me, I said to myself and then out loud, "No, I'm not a schmuck!" Stop calling me one. He did. Turns out that this was what he wanted me to say. He had a side to him that could torment us to the bone. Over the years, we'd developed a love/hate relationship with him, right up to the very end. Sad but true.

Chapter Nine: Moving On

The years flew by. At 23, my Papa died. At 33, I met my 1st wife at The Pursuit of Happiness in Liberty, NY. I was familiar with this establishment and saw David Bromberg play there more than once. He was something else. I needed some music one night and ventured out to see what I could find. It was anybody's guess. I found myself going to The Pursuit, knowing that at least I'd be able to get a meal there. I was always hungry, skinny as a rail, and 6 feet tall. The food was so good.

I pulled up once and noticed a couple of Black gentlemen dressed in their Sunday best, right in front of the establishment. I thought that if the locals were there to appreciate the talent, then I was in for a treat. I was ready to experience what was about to unfold… I bought a ticket and sat down at a good table, and ordered some food. Turned out the gentlemen outside were the entertainment. They started to sing a cappella gospel. Wow, this was going to be something special. I was an audience of one that night, until she approached my table and asked me point blank IF I worked there? No, I said, I'm here for the music. Join me, I suggested. She did. Emily Poe was her name. Hmmm.

We hit it off as she'd arranged for the group to play that night, and the only one who paid to hear them sing was me. I got her # and called her soon thereafter. She was a soulful woman, into meditation at a nearby Ashram … OK, what is this about, I thought, as we moved forward in getting to know each other? As per her suggestion, we went to a meditation, where I experienced an Ashram experience par excellence … Ohmmm… It took about 3 hours, and at the end I was spent. Ready to hear some Real music versus the chanting we'd just listened to for 3 hours.

"O-Mmmm-G!" That was a bit much… "Make it stop."

Back to the Pursuit of Happiness… Ahhhhhh!! … It's all good again, and we continued the relationship … It had potential, but I wasn't sure why? She had that "je ne cé quoi" Southern thing going on. She was from Memphis, TN, and with her father's help had just purchased an old Victorian-style house in Hurleyville, NY. About 20 minutes from where I was. We began to date and became intimate. I sensed something was different than anything else I'd experienced. Over time, she began to suggest marriage, and next thing I knew, we were getting married. She made it so, and I was along for the ride.

I don't remember ever proposing, but what the hell, I thought. We're getting married… Monte was my best man… It was 1987.

I had a sales job with the Catskill Shopper selling Print Advertising. It was okay but I wanted better. One day Emily walked into WSUL Radio Station located right in the middle of Monticello NY and spoke to the Sales Manager… John said that her description of me being a great salesperson was just what he was looking for. I was hired away from the Shopper the very next day. Cool, I thought… Radio.

I learned how to sell airtime, and I loved it. I was good at it. Bill Reynalds was the owner and greatly appreciated my creative writing when it came to cutting 30 or 60-second spots. The Station prospered, and I loved competing with the 3 other sales people. Our titles were Marketing Consultants, and Bill bought us all suits to wear every day. We were out to help make business better for our clients. It worked, and sometimes even too well. One Sandwich Shop I'd written a commercial for had to pull their spots because they couldn't keep up. Looking back, I think it was one of my favorite positions I'd ever held. The people were warm and friendly and funny as well, but after 4 years of it, Emily wasn't happy and one day suggested we move to NC.

Interesting thought, and I was on board with the idea. Now all we had to do was sell an almost 100-year Victorian house that was showing its age. Long story short, we decided to sell it ourselves and got what she'd paid for it in a depressed area and market, and after 6 months it finally sold.

I gave my two weeks' notice, and we began the move. "In my mind I'm goin' to Carolina" was something I'd been singing for years, so it felt right, 1993 was the year, and it felt good to leave NY.

I was ready for a change and found employment in Retail with a company called Natural Wonders, competing with the Nature Company. I was hired by the Store Manager named Martha, who was a hoot. Petite and super organized, she was a pleasure to work with. She'd scare easy, though, and I used to scare her a lot, not intentionally, but just because I walked softly, I guess. She always had a delayed reaction as her brain took two or three seconds to process what happened. 3, 2, 1, and she'd scream "Ahhhh!!" I always thought it was funny. The Holidays in retail were challenging, and we moved a lot of product. The company management was top-heavy and eventually caused their demise.

It was time to hit the Want-Ads again, and I interviewed for a marketing company that compiled a monthly listing of new homeowners and new Businesses as well. It was called The LeadSource, and I came on as an Assistant to the Sales Manager. A week later, he quit, and I took his position. Lucky break as I excelled at brokering leads. Eventually, the owner decided to sell, and I was out looking for work. Again !!

The Furniture business seemed to be strong in the RTP area, and

I got hired along with another young man to sell furniture for Bedroom & Sofa Emporium. Things were going as well as could be expected until this young man actually faked a robbery and tried to blame it on me. The next day, when the police interviewed me, I told them straight out that I'd be willing to take a lie detector test and would bet money that the other guy would not. I was right. He quit a couple of days later, further securing my position there. I enjoyed the business and set some strong sales records as well. It felt like I could do this for a while. Five years of NC wasn't what Emily thought it would be, and she wanted to go back to her hometown of Memphis, TN.

She left to see what might be there for her and for us. She even looked for an apartment in hopes that I'd join her. I couldn't. North Carolina just felt right to me. "In my mind, I was staying in Carolina." One day before leaving for work, she called to say that she was divorcing me. It had been 10 years, and I saw the pattern. She wasn't capable of being happy, so I said that's fine, and we had an amicable divorce. Done and done. Oh well, I tried.

She did get me to NC, and for that I'm forever grateful. "Thanks, Em."

Chapter Ten: Come & Go W/ Me.

The dating game wasn't easy. I was 45, to be exact, as 10 years with Emily had flown by. I was lonely, but wanted someone real. After more than a few bad dates, I started looking at Singles-Ads as a way of streamlining the process of finding someone right, instead of just right now… It wasn't going well. Why was it so hard? Keep looking. She's out there, I just knew it. But where, when, and how was I to find her? Where was she hiding? Did she even exist? I began having my doubts.

One night, coming home to my little apartment after yet another bad date, I was ready to call it a night. Something inside my head said, "Don't stop now. Look for someone special one more time," which was what I heard a still, small voice say. One more time, but I was tired of it all. I looked again. One more time.

Her ad read "Come & Go w/me." How beautifully simple and to the point. I had to call the number before calling it a day. I had to, and I'm glad I did. I also knew that it would generate several responses … How do I stand out? What might I say to get her to call me? I decided to sing her a love song on her voicemail… "She's a Lady, and I chanced to meet her in my scuffling day …

She's a Lady, she hypnotized there that day when I came to play in my usual way. Hey … Linger with me, she said yes, and oh the time did fly … Come let me zip that dress, and how the time went by …Oh Lady, you lady of ladies. I'll remember days that felt like it was rainin daisies" … I think those were the words back in November of 1999. It worked, and she called me the next day.

We agreed to meet on 11/22/99 to be exact. The numbers are special as any combination of 2, or 22, or 222 are indicator to me. My angel numbers. Ruth was to meet me at George's Garage in Durham… See you there, I said… I loved her voice.

Chapter Eleven: Our 1st Date

I've always been punctual, and this time I got there early. While sitting in my Toyota MR2, waiting for the hour to be right, watching people come and go. I noticed a beautiful woman walk by my car. I wanted to roll down my window and say something to her as a backup plan in case my date with Ruth didn't work out, but I didn't, and thought to myself, why can't I meet someone like her? "Why, Lord?" was my spontaneous silent prayer. She walked away, and I had to let her go, as I had Ruth waiting for me inside.

I walked in, noticing the same young woman sitting alone. It was Ruth, and it felt right from the very moment I laid eyes on her. We both looked each other over and smiled, appreciating a good 1st impression. Really good in fact. I joined her at her table.

She was easy to look at and easy to be with as well.

We talked, smiled, and laughed, as we immediately had chemistry. A couple of hours flew by, and then she asked me a question: "How did I feel about kids?" It was our 1st date, our 1st time meeting. She expected an answer. "You know, part of me feels like I've had kids in past lives and will have kids again in future lives. So for now, I'm good with not having kids," was my answer. "Shit!!" I immediately thought, realizing that I might have just said something very right or very, very wrong. She smiled and agreed and we made plans to see each other again soon. Our 1st kiss was amazing. I could see myself being with her for a long time.

The year again was 1999, and folks were talking out loud about how clocks and computers were all going to fail or worse, with the arrival of the New Year 2000. What if they were right?

Was the end of the world coming? Unnerving for sure.

I had to think and act fast, I thought. So with a deep breath and just five weeks into knowing her, I got down on one knee and told her that I loved her and would propose to her on New Year's Eve. She was nervous, but I thought she was pleased as well. Fingers crossed.

I presented her with a dozen red roses, and later that day we went off to enjoy dinner together someplace special. La Parizad in Durham. We enjoyed each and every tasty treat they presented us with, and when the moment was right. I kind of knelt down and asked her the question. She was ready with her answer and handed me a single petal from the roses I'd given her earlier. What's this? Not expecting this, I dropped it under her chair. I picked the petal up, not really sure what I'd find… A single word written there that day, and that word was "Yes." She said yes. Ruth had said yes !!

We agreed to wait and not tell anyone until the moment was right. It was our little secret, and we were happy with it. I'd let her say when. As the next few months unfolded, I told her I'd put a deposit on a new Audi TT and was really looking forward to getting it. Her comment was that if instead we took that money and used it to travel, we'd be able to enjoy a lot more. Interesting thought, and so I cancelled my order the next day. I loved that car when it 1st came out. Oh well, I must love her more was my realization.

We enjoyed each other's company in every way possible, and I knew in my mind at least, we were engaged. It was our little secret, and we both kept it well, right up until April 1st. April Fool's Day 2000. I'm serious.

She'd been invited to a Birthday Party in DC at a yacht club …

Fancy, I thought, and so we went as a couple. Her friend was celebrating her boyfriend's birthday with a surprise party. We stopped on the way for a quick visit with her brother as her Parents were visiting. Ruth told them I was distracted by something, but I knew our being engaged was now out in the open. We were officially engaged.

Her brother and his wife along with her Dad were very pleased but it was going to take a little time for her Mom to rejoice with the news. She'll come around eventually, I thought. It took about 20 years for her to tell Ruth that I was her new favorite Son-in-Law, bumping her sister's husband to #2 … It was huge.

We had a surprise birthday party to go to, so off we went. It was a beautiful location and we'd been asked to dress for the occasion. Something looked odd as there were a lot of chairs and a couple of big tents ready to accommodate much more than a birthday party. It was, in fact, a Wedding. "April Fools." Wonderful, as her friend surprised us all with what was to be her wedding day… Well done.

After the wedding, it was time to congratulate the new Bride, and so I left Ruth at our table and went over to share our good news. Upon hearing that we were engaged, this newlywed woman leaped off her podium and called out to Ruth … "Ruth, where are you?" The two of them smiled as they reconnected. Mind you, this young woman's every move and every word were being recorded and videotaped. I was standing about ten feet away when the new Bride called out loud to Ruth saying, "Ruth, are you with child?" "Ah, no," Ruth said, as I tried my best to hold back my laughter, thinking to myself that she must have been with child herself. It was a great April Fool's Day. Best ever!

Chapter Twelve: Our Wedding Day

We drove up to Woodstock, NY, to share our good news with my best friend, Monte, and his wife, Anna. I'd known him from college in 1974 at Tel Aviv University. He was a very spiritual person and later became a Rabbi and was also a very talented musician. We used to sing as he played his 12-string guitar to Here Comes The Sun on the roof of our dorm. James Taylor, Paul Simon, Bob Dylan and Neil Young were also some of our favorite song writers. He even got me to sing with him on stage once. He loved to play and sing, and make Art as well.

The day was May 1st, 2000, and before leaving, our friends there in Woodstock, they insisted that they bless us in this small town's Central Park. Every opportunity to be blessed is important. We had places to go and things to do and blessings could only help us survive the next week or two together as a couple. It was a special moment.

I'd told my soon-to-be wife that I'd grown up in Sullivan County near a Gliding Airport and that if she wanted, we could stop by and enjoy a ride/lesson on how to fly. "Oh yes," she agreed, so I booked us a couple of flights on a glider. It was windy, though, almost too windy to fly, but Ruth wanted to try it, so she went 1st and I stayed on the ground.

I'd positioned myself near a handful of other men who were there watching the takeoff. I assumed them to be other pilots as their conversation was about what they were seeing as the Tow Plane took off, pulling the glider with Ruth and her pilot behind it. "Oh, you see that?" one of them said to the group. "That's not good!" The wind suddenly blew so hard against the tow plane that it slowed during their takeoff. The glider was about 40 feet in the air, 20 feet higher than the tow plane, which was normal. As the wind slowed, the tow plane, however, the cord connecting it to the glider began to slacken. "Not good, not good at all." I thought to myself.

At that height, it could have been catastrophic… The tow plane's engine gave it all it could revving to its max. Within what felt like forever, the cord connecting them became tight once again.

I truly feel that it was the blessing we'd received earlier that day from Monte that saved her from dying that same day. I thought I'd almost killed my bride-to-be. I wondered how I would have explained it to her family? "I think I'll pass on flying today," I told the manager as she offered me a refund.

Ruth said that she enjoyed her flight… I'm just glad she never heard what I heard those pilots saying, as it was a really close call.

We continued on to visit my sister Nicole and her family, which included my Mom. It was going to be her 77th birthday, and we chose to get married on her day to honor her. Everyone loved Ruth. She's wonderful, they all told me, and everyone was happy for us. My sister's husband Mark, really liked her, my sister shared with me later. We both smiled.

On May 3rd, we flew and drove to Anna Maria Island in Florida to be married by my friend, with whom I had worked for several years, helping him create and sell his unique pieces of Art. Yes, I'd been an Art Dealer once upon a time, but that's another story for later. Richard Royce, in addition to being an artist, was a Scientologist and an ordained minister for the church. A fact that we'd not shared with Ruth's family until her sister joined us as part of our little group along with my brother Sandy as best man. It was her sister who spilled the beans, and her family wasn't happy as they were all believers in Jesus Christ and not L Ron Hubbard. We'd deal with it later, but it's going to take some Splainin' for sure.

Everything went without a hitch, and we were married later that evening on the beach with a gorgeous sunset. I'd told Richard that I had written a poem for Ruth and wanted to read it before he pronounced us man & wife. He paused to let me read: "From the moment I saw you, before you saw me. I knew. The Angels whispered, "There she is," and here you are, here we are. Together we will create our destiny, and with God's grace we will smile and laugh a lot. We will live long beyond this life and prosper in ways yet imagined. I will love you forever my darling." Immediately after reading it, I kissed Ruth. Richard then pronounced us man and wife and said, "You may now kiss your wife again." So I did. We'd brought some inexpensive disposable cameras and all of us got some amazing pictures of our day, making for a beautiful album for next to nothing. Ruth's idea and so smart, as professional photographers usually charge a small fortune… Our pictures came out great.

The next day we were off to The Bahamas on a Cruise Ship for our honey moon, and wanting to impress my new bride with my worldly ways I told her I'd be responsible for our Passports. Shortly after we gave the attendants our luggage before boarding the ship, Ruth asked if I knew where our Passports were. I said, "Yes, they're in our luggage, now 100 feet away and separated by fencing. OMG!" She burst into action, leaping over obstacles and ultimately throwing someone a $20 or more to let her get what we needed to board... our passports... My bad, as we joked, saying that it will never happen again. It never did.

Chapter Thirteen: This Is Nice

"Come & Go w/me." I discovered that meant just that. Ruth was a Traveling Sonographer and would go wherever she was needed for months at a time. She told me how she'd once worked in Hawaii and stayed a while because it was just so beautiful. I took a leave of absence from selling Furniture and went off with her to Old London, CT, for what was supposed to be a 3-month assignment… It lasted much longer, and we loved being there.

Parts of CT are beautiful. The Hotel we were given wasn't great, so when we had the chance to move, we jumped on it. A beautiful 200+ year old house in Groton became available… Gorgeous kitchen, modernized bathroom, and right on the water. It was a sweet spot. Seeing boats everywhere and enjoying some fabulous seafood as well. "I see food, I eat food." Hands down, the best Lobster Rolls we ever had were in Mystic, and their Old Time Seaport is wonderful as well.

I did whatever I could to help Ruth get to work on time and make her work life and home life comfortable. Winters in CT were hard as the wind coming off the water would go right through you… Brrrrrrr !!

One day, we decided to pick up my mom from my sister's house in Croton-on-Hudson, NY, and bring her to our home in CT. She loved it. We enjoyed some delicious food at the Light House Inn, located in New London. We drove her around and ended up at one of two Casinos and pushed her around in a wheelchair as we toured their American Indian Village Museum… She was enjoying every moment. When it was time to leave, I tried to help her get back into our car, as it was a little high off the ground. As I pushed her gently, she started to laugh… We all started to laugh, which made it even more challenging.

"Stop laughing," I said. I'll savor the memory forever as she was getting older. Living in her 100th year of life, as my sister pointed out, she had a great life, and we've all enjoyed her time with us over these many years. She was born in 1922. There's that #2 again. More on her later.

Chapter Fourteen: Back To Nc

The Hospital where Ruth had worked in Chapel Hill, NC, wanted her back and offered her a permanent position. It was time to settle down. She'd owned a house in Front Royal, VA, when we met, and her parents were living there. Every time we went there, we'd do some repairs and improvements. Her parents decided it was time for them to move out.

Colonial Williamsburg, VA, became their home. We've enjoyed visiting them and appreciated the History there. Ruth also introduced me to Bush Gardens and Roller Coasters, which I'd never done. Terrifying but addictive as well. Our favorite was Apollo's Chariot, and one day I suggested the front car. It was smooth as could be. Still terrifying, but we loved it. If ever you can, do the front car. I dare you.

We ended up offering Ruth's house in Front Royal to someone who needed a place to live and came with fairly good references. He was there for at least a year, until he almost burned the place down while cooking outside. Some of the vinyl siding melted, and as soon as it was repaired, we decided it was time to say goodbye to our tenant, and we decided to sell. Ruth's mom connected us with a realtor she trusted, and after some final touches, it went on the market on a Wednesday and sold 2 days later on Friday the 13th. Ruth was impressed with my final project of replacing the stationary shutters while wasps were circling my head. I stayed cool, calm, and collected while pulling the old ones off and putting the new ones up. My silent mantra was "Please don't sting me, please don't sting me, please don't sting me!" It worked.

We got what we thought was a good offer, but the neighbors didn't think so and wanted us to hold out for more. We needed a quick sale, and it was a done deal. They were pissed. "Fuck 'em, I thought, we're out of here." See ya.

Back in NC, while Ruth appreciated no longer being a traveler suggested that it was time to find a new house to make our home. We looked and eventually found a great deal on a townhouse in The Towns of Governor's Village. We actually got to pick our preference of floor plans and tweak what needed to be tweaked. We made good choices together and finished in record time. Our agent was impressed with our quickly agreed-upon decisions. We bought ourselves a house. It wouldn't be ready for a couple of months and so we needed to stay at a La Quinta for an extended stay. It wasn't bad, with daily breakfasts being served before taking Ruth to work every day.

I'd negotiated a pretty good deal at $1000/Mo for 2 months.

With extremely limited space, we went to a local Animal Shelter one day just to look and ended up adopting a cat that we both took too. Crazy, right? We thought the couple in front of us were going to take this small thin older male cat that had such an interesting two-tone face, so when they passed, we got him. We named him Picasso, but later discovered that he responded to Muffin as his name. Muff-Muff from time to time. Little shit as well, more often than not.

When we finally moved into our new townhouse, it was unlike anything we ever imagined. There was a round park right in front of our unit, which we just loved. It took Picasso a little getting used to, but that's just because he was a cat. We moved in. Home Sweet Home. It was everything we'd ever wanted. It was

March of 2005 when we moved in and 20005 was our unit.

Synchronicity maybe? Meant to be, I thought.

We wanted a Game Room, and so our very 1st project was to paint the garage. The tall ceiling needed to be brushed first before painting, as the beams were covered with dirt. It took three, if not four, coats of paint, as the wood was so very dry. That summer was particularly hot, about 100°F+ outside, so you have to imagine how very hot it was in the crest of the ceiling. 120+ maybe 130? It took us the better part of a month to finish. The garage was finally ready for Sheetrock. My neighbor recommended someone, and Ruth and I were ready to lay the carpet down to finish the task. The Pool Table next to the Game Room was done.

I went back to work in the Furniture business, and Ruth enjoyed her position back at UNC. The years together flew by. Life with Ruth felt like one long honeymoon… Wedded bliss. Time to get a dog, maybe?

A mini Dachshund was my 1st suggestion, as I had one once. Ziggy was his name, Mr. Zig. But we decided on a Pug and found a breeder in Asheboro who had almost 20 pups at the time that were all up for adoption. "Pick one," Ruth told me. The next-to-last one I picked up let me know that he wanted to be ours. We took him home and named him Bogie. Best little dog both of us ever had… Pugs are awesome dogs for sure.

Chapter Fifteen: Exploring The World Together.

Our Coming and going continued over the next few years as we decided to go to Alaska twice and Hawaii twice as well, the northeast as far as Nova Scotia, twice to Ireland and once to Scotland as well, along with trips to Seattle WA and California, Texas and New Orleans, Pensilvania and New York, NY … We even managed a trip to Roswell NM and Arizona … Amazing place… The Tex-Mex Food experience is one of our favorites. We also went to Orlando, FL for the Parks, and some even more terrifying Roller Coasters.

With passports in hand, we also enjoyed a few cruise ships… On our 2nd cruise to Alaska, we went with my old friend Richard, who performed our wedding along with another two couples. It was fun to share Alaska with them while telling stories of unique paths.

I shared my favorite story about selling Richard's Artwork with them… One day, we decided to go to Manhattan, NY, as we were a couple of hours away at the time. I picked him up early that day in my gold Chevy Astro Van, loaded with his work, which consisted of handmade paper. Really unique pieces with correct colors, great texture, and painted with high gloss enamels and water colors. They popped and were priced right, so galleries could see the potential to make money. We knew the business.

We were eager to show & sell in the big city that day. Maybe a little too eager, as I drove to the NY State Thruway via a back road in New Paltz, NY, and was pulled over for speeding. It was 7 am and I was going 65 in a 45… Not good… A New York State

Trouper approached my side of the van and said, "License and Registration." … As I reached into my wallet, I noticed that I'd placed a Get Out of Jail Free Card there some months earlier, in case I ever needed it… So with the card placed on top of my papers… I handed it over and said, "Officer, will this do anything for me?" and I shut up.

He immediately started to laugh. He couldn't believe what I had done and said that because I'd started his day off with a laugh, he was going to let it slide. "But Slow Down!" he added … Yes, Sir Officer, and thank you, I said, as we drove off. Richard was blown away, as was I. The day went well, and we established half a dozen new accounts. Very pleased with ourselves, it was time to head home. I took the West Side Highway and, at 75 MPH, was pulled over for speeding once again. Dare I try it again? I said to Richard, who said that I was on my own. As I prepared my papers with a card on top, I was ready for an older NYC Policeman to act as my Judge and Jury for a 2nd time that day. Before I could say anything, he huffed and puffed and said, "Ha, what's that supposed to do?"

"Not a whole lot, officer, not a whole heck of a lot," I said to him.

He took my license back to his car, and when I looked in my mirror, I noticed him laughing. I said to Richard, "I think he's laughing in his car." 2 or 3 minutes later, he came back telling me that he's going to let this one go, "But Slow Down!" Yes, Sir Officer… Yes Sir!… Off we went. Wow, right? Amazing Grace.

To this day, it's still funny because when we finally got to Richard's house, he immediately told his kids to get him a Get Out of Jail Free Card for his future needs. He did get stopped for speeding about 6 months later, but he couldn't work it the way I did. He was ticketed. Sometimes the universe smiles and laughs with you, and that was my day. Twice in the same day… I retired the card, knowing that it would never happen again.

Traveling together was such fun until something like a pandemic hits and puts a stop to it all. We'd been quarantined for the last year and a half and missed the carefree joy of traveling. Nothing quite like it, really.

Like so many, I wondered if we'll ever return to some semblance of what once was. I hope so, but time will tell. Pretty scary times these days. My cup is still half full, and I hope yours is too. I guess that it depends on which day the question is posed

1/2 full, 1/2 empty? Maybe half & half at times if possible? I'm just saying. "Half & Half" at times, it's funny.

Chapter Sixteen: 2021 And Beyond.

Williamsburg, VA, was becoming more of a challenge for Ruth's parents, and so it was time for them to move. Her brother suggested they come to live near Nashville, TN, so that he could help them when needed.

We did what we could as their Townhouse went up for sale. Cleaning & painting, along with a few repairs, became our routine.

Her brother told us to "caulk & paint and make it what it ain't." We were happy to help, and whenever possible, we did a little sightseeing as well. It went on the market and sold the same day.

"Oh, happy day!"

Being careful and keeping our distance became the norm. Anti-Social Distancing as I called it, as I noticed everyone acting differently. Maintaining a six-foot space between one another quickly became twelve to twenty feet as we all acted as if we were lepers in a Leper Colony. Everyone's running a little scared these days. Then I watched as January 6th unfolded right in front of my eyes on a Hotel TV as Ruth continued the final clean-up of her parents' unit. I'd take pictures of the TV screen and text them to her as it was "un-freaken-believable." An insurrection in the Capital was taking place in front of my eyes. "W.T.F.!!" I flashed back to when Papa witnessed Lee Harvey Oswald get shot on live TV. He was shaken, as was I. What was going on?… Anybody's guess… We shall see.

Even with inoculations, we all needed to keep our distance and wear a mask. I always felt like I was about to rob someone when wearing one, but it's expected. That is, unless you don't believe that there's a pandemic and that it's all a hoax. My old friend Richard tried his best to convince me, and so I had to break ties with him. "We're done here," I told him… One of us is going to die from this, and I'm not a gambling man. "See you in the next life." I had to finally say to him.

It's been a strange year of saying goodbye to several old friends … Some lost to drinking the Trump Kool-Aid, others simply were not the friends I thought they were … and still others lost to this Anti-Social Distancing I mentioned. It adds up to a handful or two, and I'm sorry to see them go, but I have to release them to the universe at this point.

Speaking about the universe for a moment, where do you stand on the Alien phenomena? The Alien Agenda. Places like Puma Punku are more than 12,000 years old, and Teotihuacán, Mexico, translates to City of the Gods. The Gods… I think they were more like visitors from another planet. They recently found primitive cave drawings dating back some 226,000 years. It's mind-altering if you can be open to it. "We are not alone. We have never been alone." Ancient Aliens… Yes, I'm a believer and love the many sites they point to as evidence to prove their case. Archaeology is fascinating and leaves us a hint of what once was… Hard to argue the evidence.

Other shows we watched include The Travel Chanel, Nature shows, Cooking competitions, American Pickers, Modern Family, The Goldbergs, Unbreakable, Comedians in Cars getting Coffee, Rediculousness, Mandalorian, Lost in Space, New & Old Star Trek shows, Love it or List it, The News, and of course Ancient Aliens … and the occasional Foot Ball Game when The Panthers are playing. It's a lot, I know, but hey, we're homebound… Prisoners of this Twilight Zone / Outer Limits episode called Covid 19, 20, 21… and so it goes … It's crazy.

The last movie we saw together was The Last Duel, and I squeezed in Last Night in Soho. That's it, as we need to protect ourselves. We cancelled our Movie passes. We drove by a marquee advertising the new Bond movie "No Time to Die," which included a sign stating "No Masking required." I kid you not.

I did manage to shoot up to NY to share what was my Mom's 99th birthday. We were all vaxed up and needed to be together. Glorious, as she enjoyed seeing us all happy and healthy. It was great to be together again as we'd all missed Thanksgiving the year before. We'll see each other for Thanksgiving this year, I thought for sure, but I was wrong.

My brother Sandy told me once many years ago that happiness is not a continuous state of being, as moments of unhappiness or even sadness are necessary to appreciate the opposite. Accepting this will help to get through it, whatever IT is. He's a very wise old soul… I love his strength. He's been my Sherpa / Shaman spirit guide all these years, and I'm finally grateful that he was born after all. :)

My friend Monte called me shortly after our family celebration to tell me that he'd gotten cancer. Esophageal Cancer. OMG! Not a good cancer to get my sister commented. I tried my best to suggest different foods and drinks that might help him, but he wanted none of it, as it only fueled his anger with his new situation, and he asked me to please stop. He even suggested we take a break from our friendship as he couldn't take any more advice from anyone. Not even me. Okay, I thought later then. We'll talk later, but later never came.

On my birthday, 10/20/2021, my caller ID let me know Monte was calling, but it wasn't him. It was his wife Anna telling me that he'd gone into hospice and was in his final days. I shared that it was my birthday, and she said "Happy Birthday" as we ended the call crying together… It was terrible news. Terrible! On the 23rd, she texted me that he'd passed at 2:22 am and would let me know when and where the funeral would be held.

I couldn't believe it. I still can't… My friend was gone.

I arrived in Saratoga Springs, NY, on the 26th, and not knowing if I'd be asked to say a few words, I stopped at a McDonald's a couple of hundred feet from where services were to be held. I got a coffee, sat down, and wrote my farewell to Monte Sugarman, my best friend of almost 50 years.

"How do we honor someone's life from beginning to end and beyond … It's life, and it never really ends. My personal story about Monte was about how we met. In 1974, when I went to the Tel-Aviv University's admissions office to be assigned a dorm room. They gave me one, but I needed to first visit my Grandma, who was living in Haifa at the time. When I returned a couple of days later, I was told that I was assigned to a different room. No problem, but first I had to go visit relatives in Tel-Aviv, and when I returned the next day, once again my room assignment changed. I decided that I'd better go to my room on the 3rd floor. The top floor, and when I did, I met Monte.

All alone in a 4-person, 2-bedroom suite, he smiled his unique smile when I mentioned that I too was from NYC. We immediately clicked and shared stories about everything, including our love of Art and Music. He was my best friend, and I will miss him forever." I wasn't asked to speak that day, which was probably a good thing. I later shared it with his family, and it was greatly appreciated. His kids call me Uncle Phil, as he was my brother.

"How quickly life goes by, filled with moments of happiness and pain as we are called to experience both. There are no magic wands to help us when the pain becomes too unbearable for words, only the memories of shared smiles, laughter, tears of joy and sadness that will ultimately help us get through this together … We have been greatly blessed to have shared so much along the way." My final message to my friend, which Anna read to him before he passed that night. He wished me

"Everything good that life has to offer" as his final text message to me. We never spoke that day, as he couldn't.

After his funeral, I drove to Woodstock to see if I could experience his presence one last time. His favorite restaurant, The Little Bear, had closed down. How fitting, I thought. It was pouring rain and time to go. On my way out of town, my attention was grabbed to look left at a bench there in Central Park where I'd received his blessings some 22 years earlier. I felt him standing there in the rain, smiling and throwing me the Peace sign as I drove by … I returned it and smiled as I knew it was him. "Thanks man.," I thought to myself… Appreciating his send off, as I noticed it was 2:22 pm.

I returned home to deal with my own turn of events, but first, Ruth suggested that we go to a celebration for the dead of sorts, being held in a small town about 20 minutes away. I went, but wasn't into it as my grief was too heavy to share with anyone. I grabbed a beer and sat down to enjoy some quiet. Ruth shared that there was a place where we could make a Fire offering if I wanted. With her help, she took a crayon and wrote "Bless you, Monte… Love always… The Schaefers" and folded it around some flowers and handed it to me to toss into the fire. I did, and for some reason, noticed that it was 2:22 pm. Monte was there. He was there with us. I smiled, knowing this, and thanked Ruth for insisting that we do this. It kept his memory alive in my heart for a moment longer… I was grateful for it.

We got in our car and drove away, and as I turned the radio on, we heard "Knockin' on Heaven's Door" by none other than Bob Dylan. One of his and my favorite musicians. Amazing Grace. "Thank you, old friend. God bless you and keep you. Enjoy your afterlife. We miss you. We love you. Keep in touch if and when you can." I thought to myself silently, but it was his final connection with me. Now, it was time to deal with Ruth's breast cancer diagnosis.

Chapter Seventeen: Say What?

On the same day as Monte's funeral my wife was being operated on. I felt terrible not being there with her, but her close friend was there. "She's one of ours." the nurses tell each other when it's this close to home. They take extra care when it's one of their own... Ruth was one of them... They knew it.

I can't say anymore about this, as it's not for me to share. I'm confident that she'll be fine, until she's not. Stephen Colbert once said "It's not all bad news ... Some of it's terrible!" Indeed, my love letter/text to her was this: "Most folks never come close to experiencing the bliss that we've enjoyed for about 22 years now. It's been heavenly, and know that if the going gets tough in the near future that I'll always be there for you. It's a Schaefer thing. We'll deal with the new cards we been dealt and life will continue to be sweet together, I promise." She thanked me.

A demonstration is a moment when the universe acknowledges and confirms one's connection with God. Over these last few weeks, months and years, it's been with the #222. The hour of my birth. My best friends favorite # as a Rabbi and the hour that his soul left his body. His son David pointed out that his car's trip odometer was at 222 miles that day. He showed me a picture to prove it... Incredible.

As Ruth was about to step out of our car to go into the hospital to hear her prognosis, I told her that we're praying for a good outcome. Let's make 222 our prayer # I said, and she liked the idea. When she called me later with what was some good news for a change, it was in fact at 2:22 pm that day. Grace I think. "We'll take it." Thank G-D.

Why do bad things happen to good people? It's life and our body's break down slowly but surely. No one gets out alive, no one. As Mia Farrow once said: "Life is about losing everything, gracefully."

"Love, Life, Loss and a soupson of Risqué." Stephen Colbert again... "Don't confuse me with Facts." My Papa once said, as he's always in my head.

I love a good quote. Here's a few of my favorite.

"What we have here is a failure to communicate."

"Get your mind right." Cool Hand Luke

"Vision without Execution is Hallucination." Thomas Jefferson … Powerful…

I get a kick out of how inspiring a good affirmation can be and have come up with a few of my own from time to time.

"Our resourcefulness is our only magic wand," and "A Healthy Concern is a Great beginning," and "T.G.I.F. or Think Greatness is Feasible."

- Yours truly, with this last one being my personal favorite.

What's your secret power? I can make a whole bottle of wine disappear. You? "I'm alive, I'm alert, and I feel great." - Anonymous, my go-to for many years and in many situations, is truly profound. I wish I knew who said it, as I'd like to shake their hand.

Chapter Eighteen: I'm Kidding!

There's nothing like a good joke, I'm sure you agree. Here are a few of my favorites: "I started turning down the volume on my car stereo so that I could see better."

"I spoke with a Financial Advisor last week, and they said that I should probably get used to eating Cat food sooner rather than later."

Sooner rather than later.

This next one's a little long, but stay with me...

David Letterman was interviewing George Clooney some years back when he told George that he was working on a joke and if he didn't mind, he'd like to try it out with him. George said, "Sure..." So a young man goes to a job interview and finds himself being interviewed by the owner of the company. "Tell me why I should hire you," the owner says. "Well, I'm very punctual, always on time. I'm very much of an innovator and love figuring things out, and I'm a team player, always sharing any credit with the whole team," he said. The owner next asked why he should not hire him. The man paused for what felt like a minute or two. Finally, he said, "Well, I suppose that from time to time I can be brutally honest!" The owner interrupted him, saying that he didn't think that was necessarily a bad thing, and that, now he interrupted, saying to his potential new boss, "and what makes you think I give a crap what you think?" Brutally honest! George Clooney smiled and said, "That's funny. He never laughed, mind you, but that's just George.

"We've been throwing darts at a world map to figure out where to go for vacation, and so far it's looking like we'll be spending two weeks behind our refrigerator." It's funny. "I'm on a new whiskey diet, and so far I've lost 3 days." More later if I can remember others, it feels good to laugh. I apologize for this next one, but ...

There are, of course, some really bad jokes, and I would never tell them myself, but my nephew Andy would and did. "How you get a nun pregnant?" How, I unfortunately asked. "You dress her up as an Altar Boy ... Terrible!" But kind of funny too.

Chapter Nineteen: Time Check

"Time is the unreal reflection of eternity."— Anonymous

I read this a long time ago, and it has stayed with me all these many years. I also remember Deepak Chopra saying that if you want to be a Time Traveler, forget yesterday and give no concern for tomorrow. That's it, as you're now in the present moment traveling through time… Enjoy every moment one at a time.

One of Monte's favorite thoughts.

With this said, it's time for me to make a confession as I realize that this book is more of a journal and my personal journey over the past 68 years of time travel… I think that it's important to take note from time to time, and this has been me doing just that… Taking notes… It's a good thing.

I remember Betty Davis saying, "Hold on tight, it's going to be a bumpy ride." Understatement for the day. I shared this quote with Sandy's wife, Eileen, the first day I met her. Her story of life and death is too hard to share here, but I remember teaching her kids the song Stormy Weather and as we sang "Don't know why there's no sun up in the sky" as it too was a premonition of her days ahead… Miss you, Leenie… Love ya.

The truth is that time flies whether you're having fun or not. Years turn to decades, and next thing we know, we're old. How'd this happen? Too quick… Much too quick… We must accept it and get used to it, and make the most of it… Such is life.

"Le-Chaim… To life."

Chapter Twenty: "Turn And Face The Change."- David Bowie ... And "Imagine"- John Lennon

"The Wizard of Oz" and "It's a Wonderful Life," along with "Cabaret," and "Forrest Gump" and "Saving Private Ryan," are some of my all-time favorite movies. "People come and go so quickly here" is so profound, it hurts!… "You really had a wonderful life, George Bailey," his angel Clarence reminds him.

My love of movies started early when TV went from Black and White to Color… The Portrait of Dorian Gray and the 1st Star Trek came to be. The Outer Limits and The Twilight Zone were all amazing. War of the Worlds was the best … I was hooked… TV was my friend… It was easy.

Then came Laurel & Hardy, Abbott & Costello, I Love Lucy, The Honeymooners, Jack Benny, Buddy Hackett, Ed Sullivan… The list goes on, acknowledging just a few of the greats of my time. Their memories live on even though they are all gone. R.I.P. and "Thanks for the memories."- Bob Hope

Red Skelton was amazing too… "and may God bless" was how he'd always close his show.

Music is all encompassing and heartfelt on so many levels, from Melanie to Mozart, The Beatles to Beethoven, we become more with it than without it. I was absolutely crushed when John Lennon passed, and recently, when Tom Petty also left us too soon. Heartbreak Hotel on so many levels. Their unique contributions will never come again from anyone else entering the spotlight today… It's just not the same.

My personal favorite is the Stones, "You can't always get what you want," and I did get to see them play in Raleigh NC a few years ago… Mic revealed that they'd played here once before, FIFTY years ago. Wow!… Thank you all for coming out tonight, as they all contributed to our Satisfaction… My wife and I were U2 fans, and we did manage to see them several times. Once here, once again in Seattle, and again in Chicago before the pandemic hit… They're great as well.

One day, my High School English teacher brought in a record player and played "Oh Lord, won't you buy me a Mercedes Benz" as Janice Joplin had just passed from an overdose the day before. I have to admit that I didn't know who she was until that moment. He wanted us to know her and her contribution to the world… It was important to him that we know who she was and how she made a difference… She did.

Denis Warner was his name, and he was both a friend and a teacher. He told us once that to imagine life out there in the universe isn't really frightening at all … To imagine that life only exists here on earth… Now that's a terrifying thought… Just look at how many millions of planets are out there. We need to be open to all of it. Are you? I hope so, because I think we're about to learn more than we'd ever thought possible very soon. As Ted Lasso's psychiatrist told him, "The Truth will set you free, but first it'll really piss you off." … How true.

On a final note, I quote John Lennon who said, "It will all be okay in the end, so if it's not okay now … It's not the end." I miss his many contributions. His song IMAGINE speaks volumes to all who are willing to hear his words… "I wonder IF you can?" … It was one of Denis' favorite songs, and we all sang it for him at his funeral a few years later. Thanks for the memories, Mr. Warner… We miss you, old man.

Chapter Twenty-One: 2021 Is Over... We Made It ... "2022"

A new year had just begun … I hope it's a good one, I thought. I'm not alone in appreciating the fact that the past year or two hasn't been good for many people. One has to ask, "Are we living in the End Days?" I'm just saying, it does look that way from time to time. Sure seems like if it's not one thing, it's another. There are too many very serious issues hanging over our heads, like the Sword of Damocles as my dad would say on occasion.

There is still a part of me that wants to believe that things will get better, and perhaps I'm ready to leave my own unique mark on the world. My mom used to say in French, of course, that "The more things change, the more things remain the same."

It's just an observation, but it feels like we crossed an invisible line drawn in the sand in that, environmentally speaking, I hope that it's not too late to reverse the obvious damage we've done… The younger generation deserves better, and as a governing body, we have not done our best… They deserve better… Much better.

I'm reminded of that wonderful line from the Talking Heads' song… "Once in a Lifetime" and "How did I get here?" Someone asked me once what it's like to have a nervous breakdown. I responded that in a way it was like taking a really good shit… excuse my French. This Book of mine may be an exercise in futility, but it needed to be put down in words as a cathartic work of art, "A Real Piece of Work," as I call it… You be the judge.

I think it's a Love Story… To my Papa, my Mum, my Brothers and Sister, and to my beautiful wife Ruth and to Life itself. It's complicated, and it's really about me becoming myself as I've survived 68 years on planet earth as a time-traveling being, here by the grace of G-D. Would my Papa still be proud of me?… Not that it matters, but I think he would, and I realize that I am proud of him as well… He gave it his all until it killed him, and I wish I'd given him one last hug and one last kiss goodbye, too. "Oh my Papa…"

How is it that when I least expect it, a presence comes and saves me? Maybe there's a Master Plan that decides some of the aspects and occurrences that make up one's life? Who knows and who cares, as I've lived to tell my story here and now.

One final story of his presence of being there when needed was for my Mom. She'd gone to Paris after his passing to deal with her Mom's passing and the settling of her Estate. As she was walking along the streets of this beautiful city, she suddenly felt ill and decided to go to the American Hospital to be checked out. While sitting in the waiting room, her thoughts were, "Oh Freddy, why couldn't you be here with me when I need you most?" The nurse in charge came to tell her that they would see her now and said, "You come with me and you stay here." My mom ignored it as she wasn't feeling well, but she'd heard the nurse... After a quick exam, they'd concluded that it was stress-related, and that same nurse then asked my mom if she wanted her to tell the gentleman who'd accompanied her the good news? My mom said that she'd come alone.

The nurse insisted that she did not, and when asked to describe the gentleman, the nurse described our Papa... her Freddy was there.

His demonstration of love was there when she needed him most.

All I can say is that I wish he could have helped us more than he did, but that's not for me to say. He did what he could when he could, and that's all there is to it ... He loved her and us all very much. Very very much... We all felt it... and still to this day.

It would appear that we've kept him alive in conversation these many years and for this he is very grateful, I'm sure... As are we... Most definitely.

Chapter Twenty-Two: My Mom's Eulogy... Full Circle?

As the Patriarch of our family, it is my honor to help us say goodbye to the Matriarch of our family. My Mother, my friend, my Spirit Guide. She was all this and more. All who knew her felt blessed in such a personal and profound way, because we were. She takes with her all our love.

Thank you all for helping honor Colette's memory. I feel her presence, her smile, and her love, and I will always remember her effort to stay with us, as she was 101 and three weeks when she passed.

Once upon a time, my Mum (Our Mum) greatly contributed to building our House on the Hill, which became our Mansion on the Hill over time. I'd like to imagine her there tonight in that same Mansion now in the sky, celebrating her life with Family and friends and all the familiar faces that made up her life.

Oh, to be a fly on that wall, as she used to say to us occasionally.

I knew her for 69 years, and although the first few years are a blur, the last 60 or so are not. Throughout her entire life, she taught us what Real Love for one another was, along with what a Herculean Effort meant, as it was something we do for the ones we love as often as we can. She also shared what it meant to be "Debrouyar" in French … to be Resourceful. An all-important lesson.

I have to imagine how my Dad (Our Papa) was probably smiling on the outside and laughing on the inside when he first saw Colette and asked her to dance at an Arthur Murray Studio in NYC to the song La Force Del Destino, which was to become their song… "The Power of Destiny."

When they married on St. Patrick's Day in 1953, my dad's mom was the only witness, and what sounded like her sobbing was instead her trying her best to hide what was laughter and joy … and it ended with all three of them laughing at the pompous style of the person performing the wedding that day. Truly, their life together began with laughter, when people were learning to laugh again after WW2.

Colette was once asked a question about her husband. How Strange she thought to be asked about one's Hobby. My Dad laughed when he realized her confusion. She had another "Faux Pas" when wanting to express her Condolences to someone and instead said "My congratulations for your loss." Too Funny.

Many of you know the story of her wanting to drive me to school when we were living in NYC and I was 7 years old. She had a small Renault-Doffin with a Stick Shift that my Dad had bought her. The car was parked between two other cars, and she couldn't maneuver out. I thought it was great because I thought we weren't going to make it to School… Three Big Guys walking on the sidewalk noticed and offered to help us. Without us getting out of the car, they lifted us to their waist and gently put us down. WOW!!! I told her right there that only she and I would know that this Really Happened. We would remember it together every now and then for the next 60+ Years.

Mum loved to tell us the story of her thinking that our Dog Sheba had run off one day when we lived in Summitville, NY. She got in

her car and drove downtown in the hope of finding her, and to her delight, did find her about a mile away. When she opened the car door and called for Sheba to come, Mum got out and put her in. Upon arriving home, to her surprise, there sat our Sheba at the doorstep. When Mum looked more closely at the dog she'd embraced and placed in her car, it was only then that she noticed that she was a "He".

Colette told us that when she'd taken her 1st Driving Test in NYC, she'd inadvertently put her right hand on the Instructor's left knee. She immediately failed as he leaped out before she ever got going. Oh well, she thought to herself, "His loss."

To say our mother was a good cook would be the understatement of the century … She was a Great Cook and could turn an ordinary Chicken into a Gourmet experience… From Soup to Nuts, she was amazing in the Kitchen. As kids, we used to love to lick the bowl, utensils, and our fingers. I can still taste the raw dough when she made her Croissants. Her Almond Cakes were delicious, and her Cheese Cakes divine.

Colette didn't tell Jokes very often, although she could find humor all around her… She liked to tell the one about a Scotsman Sleeping in Central Park… It was her delivery of the Punch Line, trying to do a Scottish Accent with her French accent, that made it so wonderful. "I don't know where you've been or

What you've done, but I'm glad to see you won 1st Prize." She actually wanted me to tell you the entire Joke here, but I can't.

When we moved as a family to Upstate NY from NYC, Mum home-schooled us for a year. She taught us about Life rather than from Books … The Sign of a True Teacher, I think. We also learned some great French Songs, and I reminded her of them all in her later years. "Sure le Pont, Davinion … On e Dance, On e Dance." And Mon Amie Piero, prete Moi ta Plume. Pour écrire un mot. (Excuse my spelling here) "Lend me your pen" sounds so much better in French.

Her tenacity and endurance were simply amazing, and I remember her shoveling Snow so Papa could make it home or replacing Stones from a Terrace that had collapsed … Slowly but surely and Bit by Bit, what seemed impossible Got Done. Her Herculean Effort Lesson for the day… We got it.

Mum's Maiden Name and my Father's last name both translate to English to mean the same… SHEPARD. So over the years, they managed to produce a handful of sheep. My two younger brothers and my sister, and I. She often referred to her favorite, but if you ask any of her Sons which one of us was her favorite? … We'd each have to say that it was us and a unique quality of hers. Each one of us was as special as the other.

ALADINS was a business my Parents started together in their early years, designing and manufacturing a Tiny Lighter that could be worn as jewelry. They were delighted when Betty Davis used it to light her cigarette in the Movie "What about Jane?"

What a life she lived. One to be celebrated for sure. She embraced what Joi de Vie really meant.

On a final note, a Quote of hers and one that reminds us of her unique sense of Humor, and I quote: "We All Do Strive for a Piece of Land and All Do Get IT in The End." Too funny.

She loved to see and hear us all laugh and smile together through good times and bad.

Our Papa is here with us in Spirit. He taught us that MOTHER's DAY should be every day, and since his passing in 1977, we have all tried our best to do just that. I think he'd be pleased, and I feel him smiling in agreement.

"Oh my Mama, to me, she was so wonderful… Oh my Mama, to me, she was so good." They both were.

I've come to appreciate how the mind works, or at least how my mind works… Apparently, I'm more of a Shotgun Blast than a Sharp Shooter, but the gist of my story is intact, and that's all that I'd hoped for… I like to think our story was unique.

"Thanks for coming along for the ride… It's life… It's the shit. The really good shit."- Yours truly.

The End.

P.S. If you're ever asked what you want to be when you grow up? Your answer should always be "Alive." But wait, there's more. My next journal titled "Wait for it…Wait for it." Ruth's words to me shortly after she'd passed and my 1st Miracle of Love… xoxo

Our Mum & her unique smile.

"WAIT FOR IT...WAIT FOR IT."

– Ruth's words to me.

Chapter One: Worst-Case Scenario

It's been a year since Ruth passed, and it's still hard and almost impossible to accept at times, but just like I felt her spirit watching over me when I tried to revive her dead body by breathing air into her lungs… I could feel her sense of pride and joy in me trying my best to keep it together and do what needed to be done, but it was too late, and she passed later that day.

I'm left to go it alone after our 22-year honeymoon came to a screeching halt… "Thank you for my bed" were her last words as I'd placed a futon mattress on our living room floor for her to be comfortable on the downstairs level. She'd spent two weeks in the Psych ward after being arrested for robbing a bank as her cry for help… After a quick court date, the judge released her to me on a Friday… Two days later, she was gone.

My Herculean Effort since her passing included her Celebration of Life Ceremony, and my sister Nicole told me that "I'm stronger than I think I am," and it became my Mantra for the next 12 months… Selling our Townhouse, finding an apartment and moving with my little Bogie, dealing with Lawyers and Hospitals as we settled her Estate, and just trying to remember a friend's words telling me that "It'll be okay."… Thanks, Bob, as I was able to share his final words to me with his kids at his funeral just a few months later… His wife told me that I'm a very kind man… the best compliment ever.

"Time to move on, time to get going," in the words of Tom Petty and another great loss in my life… It's life and includes death, followed by it's anybody's guess, but I like to think that life never ends but only changes as David Bowie suggested towards the end of his life… He knew and danced right into the afterlife, smiling from ear to ear.

I recently had an epiphany: Life is Love and continues without us being present… She's come to me more than once since her passing to prove my point, and I believe that she's always near, just out of reach. Over these many months, I've survived by praying every morning, giving thanks for it all, as well as reading from The Book of Awakening by Mark Nepo, as it's like having a moment with one's guardian angel every day… My best friend's wife, Anna, gave me a copy as she, too, had lost her husband, my best friend of almost 50 years, Rabbi Monte Sugarman. We'd met back in

1974 in Israel at Tel-Aviv University as I was assigned to be his roommate… His wife called me on my birthday on 10/20/2021 to tell me he was on his deathbed… I couldn't believe someone so alive was about to leave us, and three days later, he was gone.

My 1st book, which I'm told is more of a journal than a book, shares my story from my birth at 2:22 am on 10/20/1953 up to but not including any of their deaths… My best friend, followed by my wife, followed by my little dog, and finally my mom at 101 years old… Too much… But it's part of life as no one gets out alive… I think in actuality that we all continue to live, just on a different playing field is all… I've had so many demonstrations of continued life after death that I'm convinced and happy for them all… They're all healed in Heaven as my Tai Chi instructor pointed out, and while I was packing up our belongings, getting ready to move, I found an unboxed wind chime with a Chinese Symbol on the top… When I asked May Su to translate it, she was surprised and pleased to tell me that it means "Forever and Eternal" … Wow!!… I felt very blessed and grateful to know this was Ruth's message of a continued life after death and that we'll be together again one day. She also left me a cup with the words "Strong & Courageous" printed on it. Good message, but it was still an empty cup, I realized… Message received… I'm trying.

May Su is my Chinese friend and Tai Chi instructor, and at only 4'10", a giant spirit guide and a Buddhist… When she asked me once how old I thought she was, I looked her up & down and said, "May, I think you're a thousand years old." We both smiled as she told me that she's 81 years young… She knows the truth of it all in that we're born and live our lives and eventually get sick and die, only to be reborn to do it all again… She's very wise and always smiling… Always.

When Ruth passed away, I was walking my little dog exactly one week later and was able to get unusually close to a Blue Heron, and I immediately knew that it was Ruth coming to say hello… May Su made several paper cranes for me and shared that they symbolize Peace, Health & Love… My brother's son Andy had an out-of-body dream shortly after Ruth's passing and saw us both sitting together in Church, when Ruth stood up and moved to the aisle and rose upward as the spirit she now was, going up to Heaven above… A profound experience for him, and I was so happy that she was able to share it with him and that from now on she'd visit us in the form of birds or other creatures whenever she could… and she has many times.

Since then, she's visited me as a bird or a butterfly or even as a dear with huge antlers, and just so obviously her joyful spirit comes when least expected and so appreciated. She came the last time as a squirrel, and as I watched her appreciation of a chair she'd purchased for camping, I just knew it was her enjoying a moment, and even peeked over the back of the chair to appreciate my witnessing of this precious moment not once but three times… "Hello, you," we used to say to each other… Indeed.

My hope here is to simply share as many of the thoughts and moments I've encountered while trying to imagine a life without them… They're all still near for sure … "She wants you to be happy" May Su told me and once while at my favorite BBQ stand a gentleman noticed me and said "Enjoy your food and your car, as she wants you to be happy."- A complete stranger carrying her message of love and good wishes for me to move forward with my life… If you've ever seen the animated movie "UP" where the old man loses the love of his life, and when he finds her diary, notices that she'd written "Thank You for it all and Go find your next great adventure" …

I'm trying.

I told him, I'm trying.

Chapter Two: Markers For Change... You Can Quote Me.

"Life is about losing everything, gracefully."- Mia Farrow

"Love… Life… Loss… and a soopson of Riskay."- Stephen Colbert What's your secret power? … I can make a whole bottle of wine disappear."- Me

"What we have here is a failure to communicate." and "Get your mind right."- Cool Hand Luke

"Don't confuse me with/ Facts."- Our Papa :)…

"I have a heavy heart & a bad case of indigestion."- A President Johnson impersonation and my effort at jocularity at my mom's funeral… "Hey, how bout that eulogy?" … My brother's son Andy told me, "I killed it." … He's such a sweet young man and always makes me smile, even when it was just so hard.

"Vision without Execution is Hallucination."- Thomas Jefferson. "Don't dwell on it."- a line from the movie 1917… A must-see war film. My 2 cents.

"Life teaches us to stand on our own," and "It'll be okay." Bob's last words to me.

Our shared life experiences make us who we are and who we're meant to become, over time."- an observation.

"We cry out to God for something real and hope that our prayers are heard."- an observation.

"May you live in interesting times." A Chinese saying that could be a curse or a blessing, or a little bit of both… We're asked to wait and see.

My apartment is my little oasis for healing… It's home, however, I'm aware of being all alone at this point… All alone.

I sometimes refer to it as "My home away from home."

"Put your bravest plans into motion… and Action!"- My goal.

The 5 Stages of Grieving are: Denial / Anger / Bargaining / Depression and Acceptance. Sounds about right… All leading us to closure, hopefully.

"The most powerful quote of the week was offered up after yet another shooting and mass killing… It was this: "It's time to move beyond thoughts and prayers and The Paralysis of Analysis while waiting for the Miraculous."- Well said, Reverend… Well said.

"Life is a learning experience… Be open to it… Learn from it." An observation.

"Sometimes we are forced to trust, even though it should be voluntary and come naturally." An observation.

"It's the Chaos of it all that is the chemistry that makes it all work, as the chaos is the reality of *it* all… Accept it, as it's life."-

The Book of Awakening by Mark Nepo

"Sometimes suicide is the most courageous act of kindness to oneself."- My words.

The ultimate destination is Joy… and a sign of deep health… Do what brings you Joy… Your true nature.

"I let the dust settle on my porch for too long."- It's called a "Lanai" in Hawaii, and I appreciate that it's her space with me along with 3 chairs for her to sit with whomever, as I know Ruth is there enjoying the place I made for her to be comfortable whenever she visits. She's grateful, I'm sure, and I feel her there on occasion.

Are you aware of the new Pandemic? … It's loneliness I heard on the news recently.

We are forced to move forward, like it or not… It's life.

"Treat yourself as sacred, because you are."- *The Book of Awakening* by Mark Nepo

My new mantras are "I am strong" and "Let's change the subject." "We must weather the storms of life… It's your decision."- an observation.

Get closure… My trauma was the day she died… Longest 24 hours ever and still haunts me.

"The pain was necessary to know the truth, but we don't have to keep the pain alive to keep the truth alive."- *The Book of Awareness* by Mark Nepo

I am here and I am present in the moment."- an observation. I need to move from what was into what will be… Make a To Do List.

"I have 3 things to teach: Simplicity, Patience & Compassion."- Lao Tzu

"It will be okay in the end… so if it's not okay now, it's not the end."- John Lennon, and so profound.

"If you come to a fork in the road, take it."- Yogi Berra "When you can't? You must, and when you must, you can." Anonymous.

"Sometimes it's just a small piece of gravel... No big deal... Laughable."- Me when a small stone got into our RAV4 once. "We must turn tragedy into purpose"- Facing Monsters... a movie about surfing monster waves... "Hear my words... My world has changed," His father admits.

"A day with no tears is a good day."- Me

"Be happy." I hear her telling me... Easier said than done.

"She didn't want to abort this one... This one being Me."- Our mom shared this with us 10 years after our father's death, and he never let on for a moment that I wasn't his... Simply Amazing Grace, I think.

A mom whose daughter passed away at the age of four loved planes and flying... So, her mom placed her picture on an airplane behind a mirror, where it remained for the next 10 years... Incredible.

When one door closes, another opens, and I feel blessed... "Live your best life."- Ben Shapiro, my nephew. He's wise beyond his years.

"I'm alive, I'm alert, and I feel good... Not great, but good."- Me.

I want to promote and market a Placebo as a solution to anything and everything... It's in there and I might be onto something... Good to be completely transparent too... It's funny.

"Be present and accounted for... I am here... Are you?" - Me.

"It ends the way all things end... There's a beginning, a middle, and an end... Simple as that."- Me.

"Embrace and give thanks for the many Miracles of Love you have received, as you are a lucky man." May Su told me once.

"I'm ready to move forward with Faith, Love, and Uncertainty." "I will fast today in hope of clearing my mind and perhaps envision a new course of action."- Me.

"Sometimes instead of going through something, we end up growing through it instead."- Me.

I understand and I forgive her completely for ending it herself, as it was what she had to do to escape the pain of it all.... She shed her skin and had somewhere else to go.

It was good while it lasted... Incredibly good. We were blessed.

7/4/2023 and Independence Day... The world is on the brink of war.... Russia/Ukraine... China/Taiwan... Israel/Lebanon... N. Korea/USA... Crazy... Too freaking crazy.

A leaf suspended in the air somehow attached itself to her wind chime... Floating in the air and there with some message perhaps? ... It's lovely. - An observation.

"I'm learning, pain by pain and tension by tension, that after all my strategies fail, the strength of love waits in receiving and not negotiating: in accepting and not problem solving each other; in listening and affirming each other, not trying to change or fix those we love."- *The book of Awakening* by Mark Nepo.

I'd originally asked my brother's son Andy to place the large heart-shaped stone I'd brought to mum's gravesite... He forgot & when my sister asked me IF I'd like her to place it, I knew that it was meant to be... I watched her place it on our parents' headstone so lovingly and softly... and I was aware that I may be the only one who witnessed her do it... A very beautiful moment.

"This may be the coolest Summer we remember for the rest of our lives," A TV News commentator said.

"People are good for you," A Jim Beam commercial stated.

My emotions are still frayed and raw at times... It's only natural...

"Time heals all wounds, but the only problem is that Time takes Time."- Me.

"I'm taking a vacation from my problems." Bill Murray in *What About Bob*... Too funny.

"Sometimes when you least expect it, the universe gives you exactly what you need to keep on keeping on... as everything that has ever happened in our life has brought us to this very moment."- An observation.

"The daily pain we experience helps push us forward to the next great leap of faith."- Me.

"Although my eyes are closed, my arms are wide open."- Me.

I noticed how the vines beneath her mobile on my porch rail created an oval circle, as a reminder of the circle of life.

"Shed your skin."- David Byrne and an amazing performer... "STOP MAKING SENSE" was a recently released documentary of his concerts some 40 years ago... See it if ever you can. Magical.

I was gifted the poster and have it hanging in my bathroom.

"I really am stronger than I think I am, stronger than I'd thought."- Me.

I watched two little birds working together to build their nest… determined and so focused on the task as each one knew what was expected to get it done in time for her to lay her eggs. - An observation … "Life really is a collaborative effort." - Me.

"Love lifted me… Love lifted me… When nothing else would do… Love lifted me."- a church hymn.

"This is the day the Lord has made… Let's be glad and rejoice in it."- Robert Schuler at his Crystal Cathedral.

"One day at a time, as we're all just along for the ride… It's life… The chaos of it all… Makes perfect sense."- an observation.

There's always room for improvement… What have I got to lose? … 20 lbs. maybe? … - My awareness.

The weather is the yardstick for survival itself… and it doesn't look good."- an observation.

"I'm taking care of myself these days, seeking wisdom and enlightenment as each new day has something to teach us IF we're open to it."- Me.

I realize that the only friendship that really matters most is the one with your partner, your matching puzzle part… and that's fine."- Me.

"There is Grace and there is Amazing Grace… and then there's also Simply Amazing Grace every now & then."- Me.

"She simply returned to her original state of being… and that is Love, in and of itself."- an observation.

I saw a Pitt Bull dog today as I was on my walk and appreciated his face and his calm in the moment, and only realized that he'd lost a hind leg as I walked by… It didn't faze him in the least, and I thought now there's a lesson to be learned and appreciated… as we're all dealing with something. - An observation.

"Everyday is the 1st day of the rest of your life… Make good choices each and every day."- Me.

"Living is a conversation with no end."- The *Book of Awakening* by Mark Nepo.

"Let the sun shine… Let the sun shine in… The Son shines in Me."

I'll always remember Sedona, AZ as a magical place to have experienced with Ruth... The red mountains and the Tex-Mex Food and the Prickly Pear Cactus margaritas... So good... Too good and the magic of it all, as my best friend Monte told me to be aware that Magic happens there, and it did... In the middle of nowhere, Richard Royce appeared and surprised us both, and it blew our minds that day as the odds of it happening were like a bazillion to one.

I've shared several moments with Ruth on my porch, her Lanai in Hawaii, and her space here with me to enjoy anytime she wants. A strong presence was felt and so appreciated... and then her best friend Leslie called as if to confirm it all really happened... So awesome...- My experience.

On 8/8/2023, MUAI HI was on fire, and the beautiful hotel that faced the Banyan Tree, where we stayed, was gone. Barouch Ha Shem... Amen & Amen... Praise God... Always, as it's the most powerful prayer there is... Ruth knew it was about to happen.

I have another chance to make it right... Make it right.

"Don't confuse me with Facts."- Our Papa ... Once upon a time.

"Serenity Now... Serenity Now."- George's father on Seinfeld :)

"There is more good in the world than there is evil."- My brother Sandy, my sherpa and my shaman as well.

My Go-to Chinese restaurant is no more... Out of Business. Change is inevitable... It's life, followed by Pompieri Pizza after their 10 years in business... The Rent increase was too much and a sign of our times.

"As a Buddhist, I believe the life cycle continues with getting OLD, getting SICK, DYING, and then REBIRTH."- May Su... my Tai Chi Instructor and friend.

"Life is full of miracles once you stop and smell the roses... You're a lucky man witnessing so many miracles and holding on to so many memories she told me... Life is GOOD... Life is ENERGY... Life is OPPORTUNITY."- May Su ... She also told me that I'm a lucky man to feel a connection with Ruth still.

"My growth has been stunted, sadly."- My experience.

"Life has left me a bit banged up and bruised... It's LIFE."- An observation.

"I'm teary-eyed today... and that's okay."- My experience.

"Happiness runs in a circular motion, floating like a little boat upon the sea… Everybody is a part of everything anyway… You can be happy if you let yourself be."- 1st song my friend Monte taught me. Hard as it is, we must remain hopeful… Hope-filled. Delightful = Delight-Phil… My determination.

We feel both happiness and sorrow, as it should be… as you can't have one without the other. True for everyone… Get used to it. I find it amazing that she reminds me of her presence almost daily… Always near, just out of reach… I say a blessing whenever I spot a blue Toyota RAV4, as it was her car and she loved it so.

In terms of being a Risk Taker… Are you a 1, 2, or a 3? … All three at times… Maybe a zero sometimes. I recently had a moment with Ruth as she stood so very close and was just so beautiful and peaceful, and I shared without speaking how alone I was without her and asked IF we could be together again soon… Then I woke up both appreciating the moment I'd just had with her yet realizing that it wasn't going to happen any time soon… But it was so nice to see her again and so very real as well.

"I started to sing as I tackled The Thing that couldn't be done, and I did it."- Famous Amis (The cookie guy)

"The thing about having a Senior Moment is this… I'm sorry, what were we talking about?" - Me.

My paradigm shift is to move from taking care of myself to considering now taking care of someone else… But who?

The day before my mom's funeral, I went down to the river in Croton-on-Hudson, NY, exactly where their 911 memorial is placed… A couple asked if I would take their picture… I did and shared why I was there… An American Indian woman prayed for me that day and changed my perspective as well… Meant to be.

What is your Achilles heel? … I wear my heart on my sleeve. I think both Laughter and Time are the greatest gifts one can give or receive… and Love, of course.

"Good-Grief, Charlie Brown," I heard her say to me today, as if grief itself is good. I'm not so sure. Ruth loved Charlie Brown and used to start her day singing "It's Time to start the music… It's time to light the lights… Why don't we get things started… on The Muppet Show tonight" and I sang it to her on her deathbed, hoping to make her smile, but she was gone.

I've become a real recluse… No good friends or partner to share any of my life with these days, and oddly enough, I'm okay with it, as at my age, I've experienced so much and realize that I'm somewhat fearful of what the next few years will actually throw at us… Anybody's guess as temperatures rise and the potential for war continues to spread around the world… We shall see what will be and it won't be pretty… Hope for the best, but prepare for the worst. - An observation.

"I want you to know that you're a good friend, even though we don't spend a lot of time together… The times that we were together were always special and meaningful and significant as well… Thank you for that."- Me … I shared this with a handful of friends recently as a reminder of my appreciation. "No man is a failure who has friends."- Clarence tells George Bailey in *It's a Wonderful Life*… One of my all-time favorite movies ever made.

Chapter Three: "To Blink Or Not To Blink... That Is The Question?"

"It all went by in the blink of an eye... But it was a really good blink."- Me at 70 years old.

"Put the emPhasis on the right sylLable."- Our Papa

Finding someone new is a process of elimination... NEXT."- and my conclusion these days.

"The days are long, but the years they fly by... Indeed, they do." - An observation.

"I do one thing at a time and I do it very well," A young man who I worked with years ago used to say. Wise beyond his years. "It's hard to be compassionate and empathetic when there's just so much need and pain everywhere these days."- An observation.

It can take an eternity to know oneself... Imagine exploring one's family lineage to where it all began. "We all have our whole afterlife ahead of us to do just that."- My words at my mom's funeral... "You have to be open to it all, before IT ALL can appear and unfold."- *The Book of Awakening* by Mark Nepo.

"It's not a competition... or is it?"- An observation.

"I want to tell stories that deserve to be told."- An Actress commenting on her craft. Every human contact is special... Appreciate each and every one. - My conclusion.

"All things are possible with God" ... So I've been told, but we're just so impatient. - An observation.

"If we are sad or upset, it's because we're thinking about the past... and if we're anxious or worried, it's because we are thinking about the future... Only in The Present Moment can we find Peace."- My brother.

"It's the end of the world as we know it... and I feel fine... Not really though, as it's sad is why."- Me.

I lost my best friend, Rabbi Monte Sugarman, and appreciate the fact that we were friends for almost 50 years... I miss his smile and his joyful spirit, as it's not the same without him.

"Accept it and move on... It's life... Suddenly, there's no turning back."- Me.

My little dog Bogie was such a presence, and he knew I kept him alive as long as I could… His last 3 kisses are what I'll always remember. He passed on 1/2/2023 at 14 years & 8 months… and I felt Ruth with me to gather up his soul, so happy to have him once again. A moment of bliss for them both.

Even today, scientists can't comprehend the size of the universe. It's overwhelming. - An observation.

"If it's lonely at the top, then I must be at the top… and it's lonely for sure."- Me.

"I'm not crazy, just a little impaired is all."- A line from a song from long ago.

"I'm looking for a position where I can slowly lose sight of what I'd originally set out to do with my life… with the Benefits of course."- A cartoon pic I kept all these many years, as it's too funny.

"When you know what you want, it will be easier to find… It's anyone's guess, really… It's life, and we get to choose along the way… Making good choices is the best we can do."- An observation.

My most profound artwork is my collage of the American Flag… "Stars, Stripes & Strips"… "The United States of Paper."- Me. "I feel God's Hand in all of this… and that's all that really matters."- An observation.

"We all need that camaraderie of just being human and all." "Is this an exercise in futility? … I sure hope not."- Me.

"Be of life, let yourself be free."- Diane Levan, Class of 1972

"It's all to be experienced anew, like for the very 1st time."- *The Book of Awakening* by Mark Nepo.

"I release her to the universe as life continues and in The Pursuit of Happiness… I choose to let the butterfly go."- Me.

"You have got to put the past behind you before you can move on."- Forrest Gump.

"My survival instincts are strong as I made it this far."- Me.

"Keep Love Going… Keep IT Going."- Me.

"Couldah, Wouldah, Shouldah… You've got me questioning it all… WHY?"- An observation.

"Life seems so strange lately in that we're all dealing with something… It's exhausting, but it's what we do."- My realization.

My wife used to say things like: "Makin progress" and "Too funny and a half" and "Stay alive, I will find you." and "Hello stranger" and "It's a scorcher" and she referred to money as "Fundages" ... "Come & Go w/me" is what she'd originally got my attention with in a classified ad she'd placed... She used to call me her brown eyed handsome man... I will always love her and appreciate what we had together for 22 years. You really only get one True Love... and she was it for me.

She made me smile with just one word... "YOU"

"Good job, Mr. Schaefer," she said to me when I impressed her unexpectedly.

"I thought I was wrong once, but I was mistaken."- Me.

"Our resourcefulness is our only Magic Wand."- Me.

"T.G.I.F. or Think Greatness is Feasible."- Me.

"Where there's hope, there's the potential for everything."

"Another day, another dollar, after tax spendable income." and "The daily pain we experience helps push us forward to the next great leap of faith."- All of me as well.

I have an attitude of gratitude, with a bit of an attitude."- Me.

I've been very blessed most of my life and am very grateful... I pray and give thanks every day.

"I am strong, and let's change the subject."- My new mantra and no more Debbie-Downer... as Closure is ultimately a decision we must make.

"At the heart of all struggle there is a peaceful, enduring center, if we can only reach it," and "JOY is the ultimate destination." *The Book of Awakening* by Mark Nepo.

"Time to move on... Time to get going."- Tom Petty.

"My future's so bright... I gotta wear shades."- That song. "Both of my Ferraris are in the Repair Shop... I hate that."- An old commercial on TV from years ago.

"I was double parked in an erogenous zone."- Jerry Seinfeld "My Mini Cooper does 165... I lost my license, now I don't drive."- Based on a song by John Welsh.

"A bush in hand is worth two in the bush."- The great Bobbie Habin-A-Gootime-Vision-You-Vaz-Here... - A wonderful line delivered by the German character on Laugh-In years ago. "How do you say Nice Vagina in German? ... Gooten-Tight..." An old joke... Sorry.

"I'm so happy for you to meet me." … "But enough about me, what do you think about me so far?" … and "IF I told you that you have a beautiful body, would you hold IT against me? … Please."- It's funny.

"Sometimes instead of going through something, we end up growing through it instead."- My conclusion.

"Think about the actual truth of a significant relationship."- Me (But with whom?) … Who, Lord?…

"Trust and Closeness deepen from holding and being held both emotionally and physically."- *The Book of Awakening* by Mark Nepo.

"There is light at the end of the tunnel and it's Eternal."- Me.

"Time is the unreal reflection of eternity."- Anonymous. Once upon a time, I was happy, until it ended with her suicide… It broke me in two.

"I'm alive… I'm alert… and I feel great."- an anonymous affirmation… and it works if said every day… Try it yourself.

"There's no such thing as perfection, but it's nice to imagine from time to time."- Me.

"We blink a thousand times a day… along with our heart and our mind… It's part of being human."- *The Book of Awakening* by Mark Nepo

"Working on oneself is never easy, but it's all important."- Me.

"See the light by being the light."- Me.

"There's never any shame in needing help."- Me and my decision to sign up with BetterGetHelp… For a couple of months. Needed it… I think it helped… Writing helps.

"I may be years or even lightyears ahead of where you are now… or maybe it's not be the case at all."- Me.

"I've learned over the years that change is inevitable… It's bound to happen as the next Paradigm Shift will push us to accept what we never imagined possible… Unfortunately, there's no way to know or to prepare for its arrival… Its ETA is any day now… Any day now."- an observation and conclusion as well.

"Reality, what a concept."- Robin Williams … I miss his genius. "When reality = your imagination… It's Perfect, and maybe the tail wags the dog… What IF it can't get any better than this? … It's time to stop & enjoy."- Anthony Bourdain (No Reservation) and another great loss. "Hold on tight… It's going to be a bumpy ride."- Betty Davis" and my first words to Eileen when we 1st met… My brother's wife, who also passed from breast cancer.

"I am flawed, but aren't we all?"- An observation.

I'm so grateful we visited MAUI HI when we did… as our hotel faced the Banyan Tree and it was incredible to see and appreciate all the birds flying in and out… Good memories, as nothing lasts forever… The fire destroyed Maui the very next day, and she knew it was coming. She knew before it happened… Ruth knew…

Sometimes what we never thought could happen happens, leaving us in shock and in pain and having to begin again. - An observation.

"Are we all in need of a hug?"- An observation. Do we all reside in our own little private Idaho? Are we all so insecure these days? Afraid, even maybe? Everyone seems to be more protective. Keeping one's distance is silently expected since the quarantine and COVID hit… I call it Anti-Social Distancing… - My conclusion.

When was I last happy? … When was I last sad? … It's life. Breathe deep, again & again & again.

"When we face our fears in our mind, it prepares us to face them in real time."- Me.

Keep praising God… "PRAISE GOD" … No matter what… It's important. - An observation.

I still have moments of extreme sadness, grief, anger, and loneliness… Moments of quiet desperation where I still feel like a basket case, a nut job and a sad-sack… But then it passes.

It's official, I'm old… as I realize that my mornings now include meds for depression, blood pressure, cholesterol, collagen, and Coffee. "Not bad."- My Sister told me… I guess.

"Being human, we all have fog roll in and around our heart and often our lives depend on the quiet courage to wait for it to clear."- *The Book of Awakening* by Mark Nepo and I told Anna (my best friend's wife) that she helped me to live another day as today I finished reading The Book of Awakening she'd gifted me. I'm so grateful I told her… I'm here today because of it. Time to read it again and take notes. Get yourself a copy if ever you can. A daily read of just one page a day, and like having a moment with your guardian angel.

From beginning to end, it's all just so unreal... Our time together was 11/22/1999 to 1/23/2022 ... Speaks volumes... It was love at 1st sight and we both knew it... Ruth told me early in our relationship that she shared the same measurements as Marilyn Monroe... I told her I'm a lucky man as I smiled, confirming my appreciation. I noticed recently that behind the oval-shaped Circle of Life vine beneath her snowflake mobile, there's a round center within it... A sort of eye, maybe? ... The material and the ethereal... To ponder... Hmmm.

Chapter Four: Out Of Context And Out Of Bounds As Well.

Where do you stand on the issue of the Alien phenomena?

The Alien Agenda, if you will? … Places like Puma Punku and Teotihuacon in Mexico… 12,000+ years old and built to such a level of precision that we can't duplicate today… and all lined up perfectly with the stars above… Wow! … They recently discovered primitive Cave drawings dating back some 126,000 years… But, but, but you say… Exactly, I say… The proof is out there for all to see. A good friend recently said to me that we're going to see Aliens in our lifetime… I think Mark is right… No more doom and gloom, he suggested as well… No more Debbie-Downer… I'm trying my friend… I'm trying.

How quickly life goes by, filled with moments of happiness and pain as we are called to experience both… There are no Magic Wands to help us when the pain becomes too unbearable… Only the memories of shared smiles, laughter, and tears of both joy and sadness that will ultimately get us through this together… We have been greatly blessed to have shared so much along the way… Simply Amazing Grace, really… My words to both Monte and Anna just days before he passed. They so appreciated it.

I drove to Woodstock, NY, after my best friend's funeral in the hope of feeling his spirit with me one last time in a place we both loved visiting… I went to The Little Bear Cafe, where we used to enjoy some green noodles and a Buddhist Delight as a vegetarian dish… But alas, it didn't survive the pandemic and was no longer… It was pouring rain, and as I decided to leave, I drove by their tiny Central Park and I felt Monte standing there in the rain, smiling his unique smile and throwing me the Peace Sign as I drove past… No doubt, so I threw his spirit the Peace Sign… so very grateful for the shared moment of bliss. It was 2:22 pm, proving his presence all the more as it's a most profound number for us both… I was born at 2:22 am, and he passed at 2:22 am… His son shared that his dad's car odometer read 222 miles on it as well.

Coincidence? No way… Not possible.

"A Twist of Fate"- Bob Dylan

One time in my living room after Papa died, I was desperate for a Sign of His Existence in my life, and almost demanded a Demonstration from on High… I was directed to pick up a pen and paper and start writing. This poem came to me as an answer to my prayer… "What is my reason for being Lord Jesus… What is my reason for breathing, for living? … What is it really that you want me to do? … What is the essence behind me and YOU? … What does it mean "me in YOU… YOU in me?" … What did you say? "That the blind can then see." … What, 1st me in YOU then YOU in me… Thank YOU, Lord, now this blind man can see." A gift from above that day… You can't make this stuff up. Believing really is seeing. "Don't ya know."- Ruth.

I've been blessed in my life as I've experienced a handful of out-of-body dream-like moments along with obvious answers to prayer as well… My 1st was where I was flying through the air at a very high speed, as my lower body from my hips down was being pure rocket thrust… Very enjoyable, until I became aware that I was heading straight for a mountain and a collision was imminent… Without thinking, I took a deep breath and blew the mountain out of the way so as to continue my flight… and then it was over and I returned to my normal self, but I have remembered this gift for what it was… Prepare for obstacles as there will be many, was perhaps the message that day… Prepare for them, if possible.

My 2nd out-of-body experience was where I was invited to sit at a large Cloud-like table in the sky and be aware of a few familiar Spirit Beings along with a few unfamiliar ones as well… Our shared conversation was telepathic, and not a word was spoken… After a brief period, I was told that I'm doing alright and that it wasn't my time yet, and I needed to return to my life on earth… Beautiful and mind-blowing as well.

My 3rd similar experience was when driving up to NY to visit with family, and as I was distracted by something below my line of sight, I looked up, and I realized that all traffic had come to a complete stop ahead of me, and I was about to slam into it at 73 mph… OMG… Seriously, about to die and kill other innocent people as well… One quick glance in my rearview mirror revealed my dad, my uncle, and my cousin all sitting together in the back seat of my little Honda Civic… My uncle Connie was a great driver and told me without words to Turn Now and have faith that it will be okay… But do it now! With a very quick, sharp 90-degree turn, I jumped over three lanes to the outermost side of the road, where I made another 90-degree turn and was safe. Amazing Grace… and as I checked my mirror noticed that they'd all vanished as their mission was to spare me a horrible death was done… I'll never forget it… Never.

After Ruth passed away, she gave me several signs of her continued life with what my Tai Chi instructor and friend calls "Miracles of Love." She told me I'm a very lucky person to experience this. Shortly after she'd passed and everyone had gone, and I was ready to call it a night, when I heard her whisper to me, "Wait for it.. Wait for it." … So, I stood in front of the TV not knowing why, when suddenly a commercial came on with nine different images one after the other and all saying the same thing… "THANK YOU, PHIL" … Nine times !!… Incredible, as the commercial itself made no sense, and yet the message to me was clear… She was able to somehow communicate her gratitude for everything… It meant so much, and I have all nine images in my photo album on my phone to this day… "THANK YOU, PHIL" … Simply Amazing Grace.

Another time, when I realized that my little dog was in decline and I knew what needed to be done for him… I called his Vet and told them I was coming… I made a quick prayer while the two of us were in my car, asking for a sign from Ruth that what I was about to do for him was indeed the right thing to do… While in the room, as I'd placed my Bogie on a pillow to be put down, a small 2-inch label on the side of the pillow was my answer to prayer… It was an image of an animal's spirit going up and not down, and I could feel Ruth there with me to receive his spirit as he jumped right into her arms, so very happy to be with her again … So powerful and another demonstration of life after death.

"THANK YOU, RUTH." … "THANK YOU, BOGIE." … "THANK YOU." The chaos of it all is the chemistry of what makes it all work, as the CHAOS of it ALL is Reality… Accept it… IT's LIFE - An observation and my conclusion as well.

"The end of an era."- My cousin Rivka, describing my mom's passing at 101 years old… All her kids were there from beginning to end, and her many lessons over the years made it even harder to let her go… It's life, and we must accept it as she'd want us to… "Let's be happy, let's be gay, let's forget she passed away."- Our Mum used to sing now & then, and it was too funny.

I must share the fact that on my drive to NY for her funeral, I stayed the night at a Red Roof Inn… and before calling it a night, I wanted to practice reading her eulogy so as to be able to deliver it when needed… I could feel my mom's spirit with me, and it was almost date-like. As I tried reading, we both laughed at how poor a reading it was… That's one I declared to her while chuckling with tears flowing… Taking a deep breath and trying again, we both agreed that it was better but not great, and we laughed once more… The 3rd time was a charm, and I could feel her joy as she smiled and said goodnight… So very special.

Reading her eulogy at her grave site was amazing as I shared a couple of unprepared thoughts with everyone, revealing a large Heart-Shaped Stone I'd brought for the occasion, declaring that there were no stones here to be found, so I brought my own… Our collective marker that we were all there that day. Along with mentioning that our little group was actually much larger because of all the spirits who'd gone before her were there to welcome her home… "She has her whole Afterlife ahead of her." I declared, not knowing where the words came from, but happy that they came to me to be shared for sure.

She taught us many important lessons, and the most important was how to love, as well as to be resourceful as life demands it of us… Be prepared to make Herculean Efforts for the ones we love, as that's what love is. We all made our Papa proud that day with our sincere and heartfelt send-off… I asked for everyone's attention for one last time as I added a cork from a bottle of Champagne, we'd opened for her 100th birthday… It's going with her, I told everyone, as I tossed it into her open grave before adding the 1st shovel full of dirt… It's quite surreal and unbelievable that she lived to be 101 years and 3 weeks, and passed on the 23rd, as have several of our relatives in the past, including Ruth and Monte as well. What is it about that number? "23" … We placed the heart-shaped stone that I'd brought with me for the occasion, and when I noticed from a picture that it was gone, I asked my sister about it… Her answer to me was, "Well, maybe she took it with her." … Yes, I said… Maybe she did… Maybe She Did… and it made me smile.

Chapter Five: Happiness Runs In A Circular Motion...

Floating like a little boat upon the sea... Everybody is a part of everything anyway...You can be happy if you let yourself be... Oh, Happiness Runs, Happiness Runs... Yes, it does...Happiness Runs,

Happiness Runs... Happiness Runs, Happiness Runs, yes it does... 1st song Monte shared with me early in our friendship years ago.

Breath deep... Again & Again & Again. "When we face our fears in our mind, it prepares us to face them in real time."- Me.

I think we walk into heaven with both arms and eyes wide open, ready for a hug from someone we loved very much.

"Feel the movement of grace around you as it flows freely."- Me.

The Circle of Life is shaped like an eye; it's oval - My conclusion.

On 9/11/2023, and 22 years since that horrific day unfolded the way it did... People should never have to jump from a skyscraper... Many did just that. Horrible. God bless their decision to fall into heaven. The sound of their bodies hitting the ground reminded me of Ruth falling just above my head that Sunday morning...

It's official; I'm old... as I realize that my morning now includes meds for depression, blood pressure, cholesterol, collagen, and coffee... I'm old, but still standing and feeling good about what the future holds... It's life, and shit gets real every now and then. Sometimes when we close our eyes, we can begin to see with our heart... "I am the master of my fate, I am the captain of my soul."- Oprah.

Todarabah or Todah Rabbi... Thank you, teacher. In the quiet silence I hear God speak... Praise God every day... It's important. "Ladies & Gentlemen, we are gathered here today to get through this thing called Life."- PRINCE and another great loss. Grieving is very personal and private, even when shared with others. My words to my sister.

A Rabbi asked his class if anyone knew when the dawn had come. After a long silence, one student stands to say that the dawn has come when you can tell the difference between an olive tree and a fig tree. Wrong, the Rabbi says... and a few minutes later another student stands up and says that you know when the dawn has risen when you can tell the difference between a sheep and a goat. Wrong again, the Rabbi says… After a long silence as the Rabbi walks among his students, he finally tells them, "You know when the dawn has come when you can see yourself in someone else's eyes." … Empathy was the lesson.

Wisdom, Enlightenment, Truth, Love, and Miracles are all I seek these days. "Be good, and if you can't be good… be careful." I thought I was wrong once, and I was right, in that indeed I was wrong, and more than just once, I should add.

"After changes upon changes, we are more or less the same…

After changes, we are more or less the same."- CSN&Y

Little Richard created the template for the Rock & Roll that was about to come.

The day before mum's funeral… I went for a walk down by the river in Crotton-On-Hudson, NY, and as I was leaving, I found a small piece of driftwood and claimed it as mine to honor the moment… It was meant to be, and I still have it on the dashboard of my car to this day.

I think both laughter and time are the greatest gifts one can give or receive… and love, of course.

Let's all keep each other in each other's prayers… God in us is not a Half-Presence… Omnipresence.

"Thy will be done." … THY WILL or My will… Pick one. Tears are the only prayer God hears… and "Sometimes we cry without shedding any tears."-Me.

"Life is a gift, and should be treated as such."- My Sister.

"More anger does not equal vision," an MSNBC commentator said… True that.

"Sometimes, you just have to bow to the absurd."- Jean Luke Picard on Star Trek. "I'm grateful, I'm blessed and I'm happy."- I keep telling myself… hoping it sticks. Might one day. Are you highly effective or effectively high? … I heard on the radio recently and smiled.

Follow the path of least resistance, and it is always an option… My Financial advisor said to me.

I'm reading "Does the Soul Survive?" … My answer would have to be that after several out-of-body demonstrations, I'd have to say YES, it does.

At 4 am on 9/27/2023, I was sad, feeling the weight of it all (Kaved in Hebrew), meaning heavy… For Nic and her Ben, for Sandy and Marc…

and for how the world has changed for the worse. I try to remain positive and enthusiastic, but I feel their pain and it hurts as well… a to the bone kind of pain with no easy answers for any of it, I'm afraid… I question why pain and sadness seem to be so much a part of one's life experience at times, and I wish it were different. We all need a miracle at this point, and maybe more than one, even. My next dog's name might be Sumo.

I feel like I'm living in a state of Amazing Grace… Being able to ponder it all while seeking wisdom and enlightenment and love in spite of all I've been through. "Gettin' there."- I hear Ruth telling me… "Gettin' there."

"Biden announced plans to build the Trump Library… It will be about the same size and shape as a 2-person Outhouse and will offer some inappropriate reading material, of course."- My joke.

Let's wait and see… what will be will be… God's Will, maybe? …

Let's wait and see… All we can do is pray. Miracles do happen, every day… Todah-Rabah… Thanks much in Hebrew, and fun to say too.

I'm finally ready to love again as it's time… Maybe a birthday present from above on my 70th birthday ? Her name is yet to be decided… God works in mysterious ways, so we shall see.

Chapter Six: What More Can I Say?...

I'm not sure IF I'm an Extraverted Introvert… or an Introverted Extravert?…

Is it wrong to want love in my life again? … No, it is not. No, it is not… The are no small Miracles of Love… I saw a bumper sticker today saying "Namaste Y'all." … Namaste.

On 10/4/2023, I was Bob's carrier pigeon and delivered his message of love to his wife, Elizabeth, reminding her that "It'll be okay."- His words to me at my wife's celebration of life ceremony on 2/13/2022, a day before Valentine's Day… She was there, as her spirit was undeniably present, flying around the room… We all felt it… She was there.

"I don't know… I just don't know."- Max Fargotstein … My first wife's dad… I only recently appreciated how meeting his daughter Emily would so greatly influence how my life unfolded since we'd divorced in 1997… There was no real love between us, and so we had an amicable divorce, as she'd already moved out and gone back to her hometown of Memphis, TN… Thanks, Em, for it all, as had I not met her, none of it would have happened the way it did… and what a huge loss that would have been… HUGE.

On 10/7/2023, a war broke out in Israel after a horrible attack that took almost 1500 lives. Horrible… We are praying for both Israel and Gaza, as well, with too many innocent victims caught in the crossfire. Why are there always so many innocent victims, I wonder? "Inexcusable hatred" and a term I'd never heard used before… Horrible.

With my right hand on my left shoulder, I woke and felt Ruth smile at me, as we both remembered my hand on her inner thigh and shared a memory of love. So sweet. Undeniably real as well.

Wishful Thinking versus Foolish Thinking versus Thinking Out Loud … Which would you choose IF you had to? … Take your time. I think this 2nd Book/Journal is me thinking out loud. I survived 70+ years on 10/20/2023, and I lived it… "Well done Mr. Schaefer," Ruth would say to me sometimes. "Well done."

I saw a documentary "After Death" and a sign from above, and so appreciated… "After life there is more Life… Bigger Life… Better LIFE." … Accept its profound message… I believe it's true.

God tells the Jews, "You are the chosen people… and the jews respond by saying, "Would YOU mind maybe choosing someone else?" :)… IF it's meant to be, it will be… and if not… well, I tried as we all do… We must keep trying.

I told a friend that he seems to be busy with his life, and that's fine… Enjoy every moment… I guess I thought we were closer than we are, I said… That's life, and we all do the best we can… "Appreciate every moment for what it is."… He understood where I was coming from… No worries, I added… No worries.

"Sometimes we expect too much." … A great line from a movie I saw recently, where a wife is wrongly accused of killing her husband.

Chinese leader Xi might be the first panda to return to the USA.

My apartment is my Oasis, my Sanctuary, and has helped me get to this point… I feel both Ruth and Bogie here with me in spirit and so I'm staying for another year and might move somewhere else in 2025?… We'll see… NC is still affordable.

On Thanksgiving of 2022, I was inspired to text a message from Ruth and me saying that "her appreciation of the Afterlife is the reality that after life there is more life, Bigger and Better Life, and both wisdom and enlightenment come to us all." But it doesn't free us from grieving those we've lost. "Let kindness and empathy and compassion come and go naturally."- My words as there are no small Miracles of Love… Happy Thanksgiving," from the two of us. Powerful… I had to share.

I've had too many Demonstrations / Out of Body Experiences at this point to question any of it… We are here to love… Period. "Man, IF I was doing any better, they'd have to make two of me."- Kevin and a good friend over the years… I will always remember our two pugs playing together and sounding like they were killing each other, while jumping up and down like two fat little bumble bees… Bogie & Boo… R.I.P., you two.

"IF we're not moving forward, then we're sliding backwards, as there is no standing still."- Anonymous

"We're not in the Monkey Cage anymore, we're in the Lions Den now."- My brother Sandy and a great line.

My Thanksgiving Day prayer in 2023 was to simply praise God always, every day, several times a day… as Thanksgiving should be every day! … Sometimes it feels like I'm stuck in Reverse, forever remembering and reliving the past. "Thanks for the memories."- Bob Hope used to sing when he signed off.

My Mom, at 101 years old, was asked IF she knew how old she was? … She answered Yes, I'm a hundred & one, as she held up her middle finger as her final joke to us all… and on 12/7/2023 on the 1st day of Chanukah, I felt I needed to check my Yahoo News link on my phone, which I rarely, if ever, do… I immediately appreciated a story about a Newswoman who was photographed giving her viewers the bird… I knew it was a sign from above, as her timing and her humor continue as good as ever.

A celebration of miracles on Chanukah… "THANKS, MUM."

I recently saw The Oath and was moved and grateful for the wisdom, enlightenment, and love in my life. My apologies… as I offered up an important prayer for forgiveness to all I have wronged in my past in the middle of the night, and I forgave myself as well, as I'm only human… I'm not afraid of dying but might be afraid of living, I think maybe? … As I've experienced too much pain over the years, is why… I'm not Superhuman, but several people have told me that I'm the strongest person they've ever known. Blows me away as I've heard it said more than once.

On my walk recently, I stopped to write "Not yet is not yet and

Now is now." and as I put my phone in my back pocket, a Blue Heron flew towards me just ten feet above my head… It was Ruth, reminding me of her presence and good wishes.

At 70 years of age, it's unfathomable to accept how quickly it went by… What's your Achilles Heel? … Mine is that I wear my heart on my sleeve… Always have… Always will.

"I've heard it said that we die twice in this life, the 1st being when our soul leaves our body and the 2nd being when the last person we knew mentions our name in conversation."- I shared this at Joanne Bickel's Celebration of Life Ceremony and my youngest brother, Marc, later said to me Congratulations… I said for what? … He said that I'd made more people cry than anyone else who spoke that day. Too funny.

I've lived with a spirit of worry since Ruth passed, I told a friend and apologized for it… I must replace it with a spirit of hope… "Hey brother, live every day like it's your last because Today is a gift, not a given… Live it up & tear it down & burn it up."- Kevin and very wise sometimes. My 1st wife, Emily, changed my life for the better, forever… "THANK YOU, EM."

11/22/2023 and 60 years since JFK was killed… and exactly 23 years since I met Ruth. Our 1st kiss was amazing.

"IF we knew for sure what the afterlife offers, we'd all be killing ourselves."- My brother Sandy & hysterical if you think about it. "I think Trump is a demented old circus monkey."- My words… The Devil is orange, bright orange.

On 12/2/2023, I found a beautiful picture of my dear friend Monty and forwarded it to his wife, who informed me that it was her birthday… His message of love and good wishes, and I was his Carrier Pigeon that day.

"We know what a crooked line looks like because we know what a straight line looks like… and Trump is no straight line."- Tim Alberta

Glen, a good friend these past 25 years, asked me what it was that I kept repeating in my head. … His question allowed me to see what it was for the 1st time… My answer was this:

My trauma was this: After finding Ruth was awake at 3 am, I shared my plans to go back to work and, in fact, had 3 interviews lined up for the week… I asked her IF I could make her some breakfast around 8 am, and she said, "No, I've eaten enough," and I'm bad for not appreciating the depth of her answer… Followed with her saying "Thank you for my bed," as she was heading upstairs at 8:45 that Sunday morning, as I'd placed a futon mattress on our living room floor for her to be comfortable. When I heard something heavy drop above me, I never thought for a moment that it was her falling to her death… The nylon rope she'd gathered from our camping gear told me she'd planned it for a while… "No baby, no !!" I screamed… "NO!!"

I had to cut her down and blow air into her bloodied mouth as I felt her spirit watching me… When I saw that she was breathing again, I had a moment of hope and called 911… Soon there were 3 police cars and 2 Ambulances all walking in to help… As EMS carried her down the stairs topless, I dealt with the police who assumed that I'd killed her… Questioning and photographs of my face and hands led them to tell me that they were sorry for my loss, finally… I called my Sister and her Sister and then went to the Hospital to be with her, knowing that she wasn't coming home ever again… She passed around midnight, and at 3 am, I got a call asking if her body parts could be saved for donations… I asked IF she'd passed, avoiding the obvious. Worst 24 hours ever! "Thank God for His Presence in her life from beginning to end." Amen & Amen.

"How can we miss you IF you don't leave?" She wrote in her January 2022 Planner… She lived her life fully and even robbed a Bank a couple of weeks earlier as a cry for help… Leading to a 2-week stay in the Psych Ward… It was for her to decide how to end it… I think she knew what was ahead in the afterlife and was ready to meet her maker with open arms and eyes wide open… It was time to go, so she went… No goodbye ever, just a thank you for my bed was all.

I've heard Ruth whisper, telling me that I am not my pain, I am not my trauma, and it's okay to file it away… It's okay … Not the 1st time she's told me this, I should add, but I think that this time she means it. So, this is me filling it away… My next Book/Journal is titled "Said & Done."

"It's the ache of being alive that we all feel and live with… and that ACHE is the driving force of one's life journey."- May Su … Thank you for your friendship, I've told her many times.

I made a note the other day of all the songs I've learned thanks to my friend Monte, and was actually able to list 50… Fifty!!… "THANK YOU, MONTE" … So many great moments together.

Thanks for listening to my story. It's Life, up front and personal. We all have our stories to tell. What's yours?

"I'm ready for my close-up, Mr. DeMille"- Anthony Hopkins

"Ain't it funny how time slips away?"- Willie Nelson … Understatement for the day.

My time with Ruth is over, and it's just me moving forward without her… knowing too that she's always near, yet just out of reach. I write about our life together in my Autobiography, "A Real Piece of Work… My 68 years on planet earth." … 22 years together wasn't long enough… Tears of joy from now on.

The two of us in Ireland… Good times

"SAID & DONE."

Thinking forces me to write as I simply make a note… Welcome to my Renaissance into the future… Who knows what to expect?… A Crystal Ball would help… Does anyone have a Crystal Ball?

I've made some good and some not-so-good decisions in 2023, and hopefully, it will all work to my advantage as I move forward with faith… At least I was able to help my 2 brothers with some money, as life is expensive and there's no reason to wait until I pass to share what I have. Everyone needs help now and then.

Nothing wrong with it… Nothing at all.

Cave drawings in France date back some 16,000 years BC… and in Indonesia, some date back over 40,000 years BC… The prominent figures at the time appear to be Bird-Like Beings who imparted knowledge… Our actual beginnings were not of this world. We have images of underwater cities dating back some 50,000 years. Certainly, makes one think! … IT would appear that almost all of our Biblical encounters may have indeed been with Extraterrestrial Beings… But it doesn't lessen the existence of God.

Thank you for my picket fence, as I appreciate the last painting I purchased with Ruth, and mentioned that we never got the picket fence we thought we'd be getting with the purchase of our Townhouse. I have it on my bedroom wall and it's all I have at this point… Two townhouses separated by a garden with a big, beautiful tree, flowers, and yes, a white picket fence.

On Christmas day 2023, I appreciated learning of The Muppets rendition of "The Glory around you is born again each day," as my miracle of love from above, as we both loved the Muppets and still have the Beaker character on my shelf of shared memories… I actually found a pair of boots in his size and they fit him perfectly… Beaker w/ Boots… Too funny.

You don't escape trauma by ignoring it, but by confronting it… and that's why I wrote "Wait for it…Wait for it." as my 2nd book/journal… These last 2 years have been hard, but I survived and am moving forward, as there is no other option really.

I heard today that Trump seems to think that a President is above the law, even for treasonous acts to overthrow an election… How bizarre.

"Geographically Undesirable" was how my papa stated the obvious in regards to dating someone far away… True, I guess.

What do I see as my life in the next 5 years by 2030?… Time to take stock and decide what I will do at 75?… My nephew Andy reminded me that I have good genes, or jeans, was how he put it. Good Jeans… I love it.

Never did I think that at The Pursuit of Happiness in Liberty, NY, back in 1987, would in fact determine the 2nd half of my life, as had I not met Emily Poe that night, the rest of my story never would have happened with Ruth in 1999 or Bogie for that matter.

I love seeing movies on the big screen, and recently, I saw an incredible documentary titled After Death, which shares several examples of people's experiences after dying and then coming back to life… I also saw Napoleon and Poor Things and Men in a Boat and The Color Purple and American Fiction and ORIGIN… which blew my mind and is a must-see to understand how we, as a people, have placed each other in different social classes all over the world from the beginning of time… The Taste of Things was a delicious film about fine dining and, of course, a love story… ONE LIFE with Anthony Hopkins was an amazing glimpse into one man's mission to save so many children from certain death during WW2… I think he saved over 660 precious children. He's such a great actor and played it so beautifully.

The News these days doesn't make it any better, but just continues the sequence of it all… What a crazy world we live in with more division than ever… Not sure what will come of it all when historians document it when it's over? … ALL OVER.

Are we really going to consider a rapist, a blond mass murderer who's out for revenge, as a serious candidate for President? … Ruth used to sometimes say, "We're doomed," and she might be right … Trump must be stopped… Crazy is as crazy does.

Did you know that the most appreciated and revered car ever made is the Model T Ford… and the second is the Mini Cooper… Ruth guided me to find one that we both admired at a Car Show in 2019, but couldn't afford… BMW and The Ultimate Driving Machine… I love it, and it's the ultimate gift from above.

I think that sleep reconnects us to the Cosmic-Slumber we all come from… Sleep on it.

I need to be open to something new and someone new in my life… But who?

"There is nothing more important than Common Sense."- Tom Hanks

On 12/31/23, I told a friend who was celebrating his birthday that the "123-123" sequence would never happen again. I marvel at the beauty of life when intertwined with/ God's Presence.

Did you know that fake eyelashes are called falsies, the same term for fake breasts… I hate them both… Equally.

Happy New Year in 2024, and hoping for more… Wisdom, Enlightenment, Truth, Love, and Miracles, I told my family. What's your fondest memory? … Meditate on it until it makes you smile.

What's coming next? … Divine Intervention, maybe. One can only hope.

I found a round black & white Yin-Yang button and noticed this image again later while driving by a Vet's office… My miracle of love to end the year with… "Gift it to Andy on his birthday." I heard her whisper… So I did just that… and after picking up my mum's miniature lighter and making a prayer, my attention was moved to a 1" small Alien figure she'd gifted me once as a sign of her continued presence and joy and appreciation. "THANKS, MUM."

The significance of Jan. 2nd, 2024, and the 1st anniversary of Bogie's passing, and I finished writing my 2nd book/journal, "Wait for it…Wait for it." and was reminded that Joy is the ultimate destination… I've received undeniable miracles of love from mum, papa, Ruth, Bogie, and even from Monte's Rachel sharing his Mandolin with me… I shed a tear of joy and told myself Tears of Joy from now on.

The next day, I went to see The Color Purple and so appreciated a line saying, "Maybe God is trying to tell you something?" … Could be, as I smiled in agreement.

Jan. 6th & 4th anniversary, and questioned why we're not calling it by its real name? … The 2nd American Revolution… We really need to stop pussyfooting around using the word Traitor and say it to Trump's face… Hang the S.O.B. … As General Washington surely would have.

I'm reminded of a French expression, "Tromp-L'oil," meaning to fool the eye… Yes, a Coup is a Coup and a Traitor is a Traitor.

The Reverend Al Sharpton quoted words from a Bob Dylan song, saying that you can't fool all of the people all of the time.

I want you to learn a new habit today… Try saying "I trust you, Jesus" in response to whatever happens to you today and every day from now on… Feel your heart unfold… You are blessed.

View events in your life through the Light of God's universal presence… Rely on Him/her and begin your journey of profound reliance… A Faith-Walk with G-D… Who you are is enough… More than enough.

Bill Murray had some great advice in his movie Baby Steps… "Take a vacation from your problems." … and in Groundhog Day, his remark to his love interest was that he knows what to say when she doesn't have the words… He tells her that "He doesn't care if he's happy tomorrow or for the rest of his life, as all he knows is that he's happy now." … Wow !!… Well said.

"Anything different is good," and "Stay, Stay," he tells her in their bed.

I reminded my youngest brother, who's been suffering with Parkinson's these past 10+ years… That we are Spirit Beings having human experiences… but his discomfort is too much to appreciate what I was trying to help him understand… Such a terrible disease.

On 1/7/2023 and a year ago since Ruth decided to rob a Bank with a razor blade and a note… I dreamt that we were enjoying a moment together, seated at a round table, enjoying drinks, smiles, and thoughts, without ever speaking a single word. "Time to stop seeking compassion and empathy and instead start seeking affection and emotional gratification," was her message to me, and yet another miracle of love… Thank you, darling… Message received.

President Biden's State of the Union address highlighted Democracy versus Demo-Crazy. IF one's eyes are windows to the soul, then looking into Trump's eyes makes me wonder IF he even has a soul? … I don't think he does… Pure Evil… Bat-Shit Crazy!!… Looks like the Republican Party has become an evil enemy of the United States, determined to destroy it all… But WHY? … What the hell is in that Cool-Aid they're all drinking? … Beats me… Presidential Buffoonery as the lights are on but nobody's home. How does a demented old circus monkey and convicted rapist, a convicted scam artist in the NY Court, along with an about to be convicted Traitor in

GA, still remain on the ballot to run for the highest office of the land?… As if selling gold-colored sneakers and Bibles will save his sorry ass? "He's running to stay out of jail," and "Isn't it past your jail time? "Jimmy Kimmel commented at the Oscars ceremony.

I'm determined to make better choices regarding my health with good supplements and better choices like drinking V8 every day as well… We are what we eat and drink, I think.

I also pray every morning, asking God to make me a blessing to someone I haven't met yet or to someone I know who needs to be reminded of God's presence in their life.

God is not a half presence and there's never anything wrong with needing help.

We experience unconditional love from our dogs, and it makes me think, as Dog spelled backwards is GOD… Ruth visited me 3 times over a 2 day period coming as a skinny little squirrel to enjoy her cloth Camping rocking chair, rolling around on it and leaving me speechless as it stood to peek over the back of the chair to look right at me just 3 feet away… and on the 3rd day a squirrel's shadow silhouette reflected on my window while it was jumping to the other side… of life maybe and another miracle of love… Her departure for now, as she's free to explore and transition to wherever she needs to go next. She's free to move about the cabin of her afterlife, I thought to myself, grateful to have witnessed it all… Truly amazing at times.

We lost 2 Navy SEALS recently, as protocol says that if one goes under, then the other must go after him… God bless them both… I told my brother that I was a Navy SEAL, and he agreed.

I realize that my home away from home, as I sometimes call my apartment, is now my home, and I feel very blessed to be here. I truly believe Ruth guided me to find it as I needed her assistance… She also guided me to find my Mini Cooper as I couldn't keep driving what was her car… An electric storm blue Toyota RAV4 and she said that it was the best car she'd ever owned… I feel the same way about my mini as we'd both seen it at a Car Show in Raleigh back in 2019, but it was too expensive to consider back then… Mine happens to be a 2019 model and looks and feels brand new… Thank you, darling.

1st feedback on my 2nd book/journal WAIT FOR IT came from my mom's caregiver during her final years… "Hey Philip, I just finished reading your book and I realize that it's about your journey… I'm happy you wrote this, as it can be a great help to so many who have gone through similar things… I saw the good times and the sad, and I hope you hang on to the good times and good things you shared with your wife… I also pray that you will be healed in whatever area you feel broken… You did the right thing and I applaud you for speaking your truth."- Alecia … "Life is a journey we are asked to experience and appreciate… I'm glad you came along for the ride," was my answer to her, and I added Tears of Joy from now on.

"Very moving and deeply thoughtful," Glenn responded back to me as well.

"Thought-provoking," and "Very intimate,"- from my brothers.

"God made a dictator." AD came out today. "IF the man is unfit, we must ask him to quit."- But no one has… Why not? "Stop this make-believe Buffoonery, as a Traitor is a Traitor. "A false narrative is a false narrative and a Coup is a Coup." … It's beyond belief at this point.

I think men should start wearing fake eyelashes so women can finally see and realize how ridiculous they look… They're sometimes called falsies for a reason. My 2 cents.

An epiphany isn't an epiphany until it is shared with someone and more fully appreciated.

My 2nd book/journal, "Wait for it…Wait for it," was about my last 2 years without Ruth and my best friend Monte and my Chinese pug named Bogie… and my mom who lived to be 101 years old and 3 weeks… On Hanukkah, 12/7/2023, I was inspired to check my Yahoo News link on my phone and something I never do… and on this 1st day of the celebration of miracles, I found an article mentioning a Senior BBC newswoman caught giving the finger to a camera on live TV… It was our mom somehow communicating from beyond that she's fine… They're all fine, praising G-D and celebrating life.

I'm not sure if I'll ever feel normal again, but when have I ever felt normal? That was my awareness and conclusion. We must forgive ourselves eventually. "From moment to moment we discover the entire truth."- Sigmund Freud… Anthony Hopkins was great in this role as well.

"You have experienced so much but have moved forward in a way that all those who care about you would have wanted," Glen told me on the 2nd anniversary of her passing, and it was so unreal as I've experienced each day of it without her. She's always near yet just out of reach, as I so appreciate every visit she's offered me… Be it as a blue heron or a big beautiful buck just off my porch, or a butterfly, or the smallest of birds perching on her wind chime, as if her spirit was returning home. You can't make this stuff up, and I've been blessed with many similar Miracles of Love as my 82-year-old Chinese friend calls them … May Su is her name, and a good friend these past couple of years.

One's Epiphany must eventually become a paradigm shift…

"We're on a mission from God," The Blues Brothers once said. I became as strong as I needed to be to survive. We do what we must do, and we do it well… or at least the best we can.

Sometimes I feel like asking my youngest brother if he's vegetating or educating or just chilling, but I don't want to upset his apple cart, so I feed him what positive thoughts I can each day. Parkinson's is a horrible disease. No cure in sight.

We must connect to a higher power for strength and comfort. "According to what I believe, your future life will be judged by all your conduct in this life. Good karma is what we need to cultivate."- May Su … I'm reminded of a Paul McCartney lyric "And in the end the love you take is equal to the love you make." … I think he's right. Ruth took her own life at 8:45 am on the 23rd of January 2022… A Sunday… I reminded my sister and said, "I was there." … She agreed.

"Hello, you," Ruth used to say to me every now & then… and I'd say it back to her. We're asked to accept whatever comes our way in life and simply grow through it.

On 1/23/2024, I realized that I'm at peace with it all, as it only took 2 years, but I focus on the good times we shared and feel blessed to have had them with her… My words to friends and family, and my Sister's response were "Yes, you were blessed, as so many people never get to experience what you had. Glad you're at peace. You've done amazingly well." … I'm glad she thinks so.

Sometimes we think out loud without saying a word… I survived the hardest of times after enjoying the best of times.

"You know it's not the same as it was, as it was, as it was."- I love that song, as it strikes a nerve.

"ENGAGE"- Captain Picard commands…

"Yes, God works in mysterious ways… but who am I to judge?"

"Road Island is neither a road nor an island… Discuss."- Mike Myers on Coffee Talk

"Would you like me to have a one-sided conversation with/ myself that you can listen in on?"- Sarcasm. :)…

I'm pretty sure there are no iPhones in Heaven.

I remember being at Ruth's house in Front Royal, VA, and her asking me if I knew how to chop a tree down and make it fall exactly where it needs to go… I told her I could, as I'd done it before… She doubted me and insisted on tying a rope around it to help direct its fall… She wrapped the rope around herself, and as I was about to make my final cut, I stopped to tell her that it would snap her like a twig, and she had to trust me… It was hard for her to let go, and when the tree fell where it needed to go she was so pleased and surprised. It was her need to control the outcome and a good lesson that made us both smile. Letting go is hard… So hard sometimes as we all struggle with letting go.

What comes next is anybody's guess, and I'm open to it all and praying for God's Will versus my will at this point…

"Make sense more common."- Bill Maher

"That wasn't me," Ruth would say after she'd farted.

IF we can't help our brother, who can we help?

Loving oneself takes courage… Loving someone else is all-important as well, though.

"Pathological Narcissism" … A term I just heard as Trump knows that he's neither stable nor a genius. He'll go down in history as being nothing more than a loud political fart.

"It's not about the next acquisition, as it's more about the final inquisition."- where we'll have to answer for all the stuff we collected over our lifetime and my awareness at this point in my life… You can't take any of it with you… Love is all we get to take.

I saw the movie version of ORIGIN… Caste systems and the origin of our discontent, and some who are referred to as untouchables… Horrible and so wrong, and yet we've always done it… WHY?

I remember taking a scalpel from her bathroom and placing it in my nightstand, thinking that IF I ever needed it, I'd know where one is… and sure enough, not long after, I needed it to cut her noose and lay her body down in hope of reviving her… An un-fucking real moment in time… Worst 24 hours of my life.

On 1/23/2024, May Su told me to "Enjoy whatever you get and let it go when you must… Life is impermanent." … Understatement for the day, I told her, as it's been 2 years since Ruth's death.

TRUST… as Love = Miracles and Miracles = Love… She came again, I believe, as 2 small love birds with one perched on her snowflake mobile and the other on her wind chime… and both looking straight at me as a reminder of the Chinese Symbol on the chime that Ma Sue had translated to mean Forever and Eternal… The birds' look was so deliberate, communicating her continued presence and her current state of happiness and wellbeing as well… Good to know…. Thanks much.

My tears of sorrow are disguised as tears of joy & vice versa these days. Her final message was Peace, Health, and Love.

I think our papa was indeed a Holocaust survivor, and we must honor all those lives lost in that horrible time… Too many were taken, as we lit a candle in their memory… 6 million… More really.

I somehow knew that Ruth would pass before me, as she had a heart condition and was on so many meds for things she kept secret from me. She chose to go her own way without me that day… It was her decision to make as I'd tried to convince her otherwise, but to no avail, as she'd made her decision… It was time to go.

So significant and profound and appreciated as well, as even the smallest miracles are still miracles after all… I've been gifted so many and remain thankful and humbled by it all. Being true to oneself is to step forward in faith with gratitude, knowing God is in charge. My heart and my spirit have been broken, but I'm on the mend after being broken in two… Split down the middle.

"Trump recently took another I.Q. Test and this time broke 2 crayons."- Me.

He's both naked and numb to his own misbehavior as he now lies constantly about everything.

He's launching a new Fundraising campaign with a goal of reaching $500,000,000 and will be called their Rope a Dope Campaign… I think Biden should start wearing a blue cap that says "Make America Regret Again."

On 6/27/2024, we shall see how it goes for them both… Debate versus De-Bait… Ain't gona be pretty.

Meditate on it until the glow of life presents itself as its own reward… Peace, Health, Love.

My life with Ruth really started with her assignment to New London, CT, and Old Mystic Seaport were our backyard experience, and the best lobster rolls were our go-to… The best. I have a tower of memories in my bathroom to both appreciate and honor its significance. She'd given me Carte Blanche to buy whatever made me happy before leaving, and I created a sort of totem pole as a reminder of that time 25+ years ago in 2000… True Love.

On 1/29/2024, I realized that I'm at peace with it all as it only took 2 years, but I focus on the good times we shared and feel truly blessed to have shared so much with her… She's alive and well, looking down, smiling, and so thankful we did so much together… Give thanks for being human and be changed by the journey… Have good thoughts as often as you can, I hear her whisper… I'm trying to tell her… I'm trying.

What's coming next, I wonder? … Divine intervention may be as the world has gone mad with too many innocent victims caught in the crossfire… Far too many.

My new product suggestion is a MAGA-MELTDOWN M&M with a Bitter Chocolate center and no shell, and so yes, they will melt in your hands… Might call them a Swift-Kick from Taylor.

Ruth woke me with a kiss after a brief afternoon nap, and it was a good kiss… A wet kiss that reminded me of our 1st kiss after our very 1st date and the icing on the cake, as we both appreciated it so very much… Her kiss goodbye is important because I never got to kiss her goodbye, which is why… "Amazing… as after 2 years you finally got to say goodbye in such a sweet way with/ her," May Su told me. "How sentimental you are… I need some of that… Hope you find the right partner to share time with, as Ruth would have wanted that for you, I would guess."- Glenn Simon commented.

I must make a Herculean effort to be healthier... or else. 2/2/2024, and my monies are invested and available after I'm gone, with Sandy being my P.O.D.

I start my day with a tear of joy, grateful for all I've received, and I thank God Almighty for it, and Ruth as well.

Good to meditate and pray every day, as each and every day is an opportunity to do a little better than the day before.

"Did you stop? ... Stop what? ... Trying."- A powerful and intimate question posed by a dying daughter to her mom in the movie TUESDAY... A parrot was the angel of death, and Julia Louis-Dreyfus was awesome... See it if possible... You'll be blown away... "Everybody dies the parrot shared so beautifully... No one lives forever."

"Fix your eyes not on what is seen, but on what is not seen and verbalize your trust in God."- *The Book of Awakening* by Mark Nepo.

"If you don't have a good memory, you'd better have a good pair of legs."- Our Mum.

"Straight to the heart of the matter and every step of the way" are two phrases I'm reminded of as they reflect one's in-the-moment mindset, I think... To ponder.

"We learn by going where we have to go... It is the path off the path that brings us closer to God."- *The Book of Awakening* by Mark Nepo.

I've come to realize that sometimes change is for the better... "You have been weighed, you have been measured, and you have been found wanting."- A Knight's Tale and a great quote.

I think suicide is the ultimate example of being in the moment and being present in the now... With nothing left to lose, one decides to exit stage left... Trust is a must that indeed there's something wonderful waiting... I think we somehow know it. Fingers crossed though... What if we're wrong is of concern.

It looks like the next pandemic might be the potential for a Dictatorship in this country...

"A Republic IF we can keep it."- Ben Franklin said once. Indeed. I've come to the conclusion that Trump is the quintessential Dip-Shit... No doubt about it.

I guess the flu shot doesn't make one immune to prosecution.

Dumb-Ass...

I dreamt Ruth and I found a Gorilla, and took care of it for a few days before returning it to its owner. What would Sigmund Freud say? I can't help but wonder.

I've burned all my bridges in regards to sharing anything more about Ruth and me at this point, as there's no one left who cares to hear anymore about it. Understandable, but hard to accept… Thanks for listening for as long as you did, I told them.

I'm done, and maybe you shouldn't read my 2nd journal, Wait for it… as I've struggled to keep my wits about me and clearly have lost some along the way… Writing helps but doesn't change any of it… I shared it with some friends once.

There's a big difference between sharing someone's grief versus bearing it.

Where there's hope, there's the potential for miracles… TRUST. My epiphany… Boldness has magic to it… Be bold!!

2/8/2024 and my brother's birthday and 68 years young… I have known him a very long time… Our Papa's 1st born and my parents' little secret… They kept the fact that he wasn't my biological father from us, and they never let on. It's too funny and honorable. If I hadn't been born, I think he would have never come along later, as my birth laid the path for him to be born two years later… Amazing Grace, if you think about it.

I mix and drink a healthy protein drink from a cup that reminds me to "Get on the path and Stay on the path." … Make Good choices whenever possible.

"IF The President isn't above the law, then what's the point of being President?" and something Trump would say but never did… But you know it's what he believes to be true.

"Don't make the thing in the way be The Way… Go around it."- *The Book of Awakening* by Mark Nepo.

We're reminded that it was 60 years ago that The Beatles first appeared on The Ed Sullivan Show… Unbelievable as it seems. Tucker Carlson interviews Putin in Russia… Really? … How do you say WTF in Russian? … Putin mocked him afterwards, saying that he's not too bright… "Pretty stupid, actually." … Ah, yeah.

I pray every morning with my fingers on my papas' medusa, and then I make another prayer, holding my mom's miniature lighter she made way back when… Ruth led me to find a photo of a beautiful and colorful bridge in our computer album as one of her 1st miracles of love and to appreciate how she now has it in heaven above… It makes me smile, as I realize that after life, there is more life, bigger life, and better life.

A conclusion shared from the movie AFTER DEATH and eye-opening to say the least… We are spirit beings having human experiences.

Life is one continuous conversation… Engage or not… It's important to stay with it was my 2 cents to my youngest brother… Be more open to it was my advice to him, as he doesn't make any effort to communicate lately… He told me that he's always been this way, but I see his Parkinson's getting worse and taking him from us. I hope you'll keep reading my journal "Wait for it…Wait for it." I told him, as it's only 23 pages long and shares many thought-provoking observations and quotes that might lift your spirits, I told him… IF you can or want to? … It's for him to decide, as he doesn't read at all.

"Collaborate with God and experience peace that overpowers the darkness."- *The Book of Awakening* by Mark Nepo.

I do have some romantic regrets, and the one who got away might have been Lidia Picorra, as I didn't follow through with her… My bad and my loss for sure. I also wish I'd never met Nancy Breslow, and I also miss what might have been with Carole Garceau in Montreal had I been able to return to be with her in 1976 at The School of Art & Design… My dad could no longer afford it and needed me to find a job to help support our family at the time, as his business was failing… "Destiny is Destiny," and some things are simply not meant to be.

"The deepest things are intangible: Love, Doubt, Faith, Confusion, Peace, Wisdom, and Passion… What are they

They shape our life… Seeking love, we become love, and wanting to know G-D, and suffering long enough, we become G-D." *The Book of Awakening* by Mark Nepo.

Ruth owned a Husky before we met, and Luka was her name… On 2/11/2024, I believe she came to me as a long-haired husky and gave me 3 kisses… Her name was Charge and belonged to a couple I met outside a Jersey Mikes who owned the all-electric BMW version of my Mini Cooper.

It reminded me of her presence at my closing on our Townhouse to the person Ruth wanted to have it at a special low price just for her… As I left the lawyer's office, I met a gardener named John who shared with me that he was a Baptist… and offered me his prayers that day… John the Baptist… and simply Amazing Grace that day with her blessings and God's Grace… Both Ruth and Monte were there as well, flying around, and so happy on 3/22/2022.

"I have just 3 things to teach: Simplicity, Patience, and Compassion."- Lao Tzu … 6th Century BC.

I've always thought that living in a Tiny House or an RV might be cool, but now I appreciate my apartment being about 900 sq. ft. and twice as big. Perfect and hard to imagine any less, as most Tiny Houses are about 400 sq. ft. and too small, I now realize.

Ruth was my Valentine for 22 years, and I think that you only get one true love in one's life.

About a week before Valentine's Day in 2024, a skinny little squirrel visited my porch not once or twice, but 3 times to enjoy the canvas rocking chair she's purchased for camping but never got to use… It rolled its little body so playfully appreciating its texture and once even stood up and turned to look right at me, just 3 feet away, watching… Fearless and so lovely. On Valentine's Day, a similar squirrel came to my glass porch door with an acorn in its mouth, tapping three times to get my attention. You can't make this stuff up, as miracles of love are just that profound and heartfelt. "Thanks for coming and going w/me" was her message that day… From beginning to end, as she originally said, "Come & Go with me," in a Singles AD she'd placed that got my attention back in 1999… Beautiful.

A Renaissance is coming soon, as I saw "ONE LOVE," the Bob Marley movie… "Don't worry, bout a thing… Cause every little thing gona be alright." … "Sometimes the messenger must become the message," his wife tells him. Very moving and a powerful spirit in the music world. I was never into Reggae Music, and I'm sorry I missed out back then, I now realize.

My tears of joy continue to mask my tears of sorrow and vice versa… "Courage is Grace under fire."- The Color Purple made its point very clearly…

I'm in a JC state of mind these days and appreciate how simply saying or thinking "Praise God" is indeed the most powerful prayer there is… I say it several times a day these days.

A vote for Trump is a vote for self-destruction… "They're two grumpy old men," Nikki Halley told us and added that she won't be kissing King Trump's ring any time soon. She changed her mind, though, after pulling out of the race. Hoping to be his V.P., maybe?

I remember our mum singing "On the Road Again," and her smiling face when she did.

Ruth's snowflake mobile was reflected in the glass door, and the morning sun was shining on my face, reminding me of her continued good wishes and love… Grace once again.

I think God has the ultimate sense of humor… as I notice an eye label on my glass door.

I wonder sometimes if there's a Lost & Found in Heaven as I've misplaced some precious items in my day… My Mum's clay Neanderthal Sculpture, along with the Silver Spoon she'd gifted me once… A drawing I did of a Spiral Staircase for a class project at The School of Art & Design in Montreal… My Grandfather's gift of a 24K gold ring (Herman)… and the heart-shaped stone we left on my parents' headstone… Maybe she took it with her my sister told me. Funniest thing she ever said. Maybe she did,

I responded… Maybe she did.

T.G.I.F. or "Think Greatness is Feasible"- My words and interpretation… A reminder to myself… "Happiness is continuing to desire what we already have."- The Taste of Things … "It's not about having what you want, it's wanting what you have." Sheryl Crow… My sister reminded me… "Don't let me get too deep" is another great line of hers.

Pathological and F'd Up… in relation to it all, as Trump is fined almost half a Billion Dollars in NY and 85 million for losing his rape case… He'll never pay a dime of it.

"Les goûts et les couleurs on ne peut pas les discuter." – My Mom "Love lifted me… Love Lifted me… When nothing else would do, Love lifted me."- A Church hymn.

I still tear up at times, unsure if they're tears of joy or tears of sadness. … Can't fool me.

I'm pushing forward through the muck, searching for clarity and love, IF possible. "Hello stranger"- Ruth used to say to me every now & then… I found a Card she'd written me once, saying "You, You, You… Thank you for all the grand adventures we have shared together in so many ways… You are such a wonderful life partner … Love you so very much."- Your Wiff, she signed it.

So awesome.

"Stop The Squeal."- My words as Trump lost… Period… No amount of endless squealing about it will ever change the end result… What a loser.

Every decision I've made in my life has brought me to experience it all, and changing any of it would have changed everything that happened along the way… In The Pursuit of Happiness in Liberty, NY, where I met Emily Poe and spent 10 years with her, which ultimately led me to find Ruth, and share the blessed 22 years I had with her. "Makin Progress." I hear Ruth telling me… "Don't ya know."- Her words, as well, that still make me smile.

IF we have them in our heads, then we have them in our hearts… "Still a man hears what he wants to hear and he disregards the rest."- Simon & Garfunkel

On 3/23/2024, two years, two months, and two days, and I'm still mourning her death… Aware of the number 222 as it's always been so significant and meaningful in my life… She knows.

I need to feed my mind so as to heal my heart, as I've become a real recluse and no longer the Rolling Stone I used to be… I try to focus on and remember the good times.

"Pain is inevitable, but suffering is optional."- *The Book of Awakening* by Mark Nepo.

It's time to move past it and towards a New You experience.

I noticed a fat little bird perched on her wind chime… "Hello Stranger." I could hear her say… Thanks for stopping by I said. I must summon the courage to make the act of living essential again. I'm reminded of a song by K.D. Lang "Calling All Angels… Calling All Angels." … Indeed.

Being treated like a Queen or a King is overrated…

Two testicles sitting together, and one turns to face the other and says, "Hi, my name's Trump, what's your name?" … The other testical says, "My name is Johnson, what's yours?" … It's funny.

Real moments of joy are few and far between… I still feel her with me in our bed, along with Bogie, as night-night was his favorite time of day… He loved being on our bed, even in hotels… and loved pillows, so I placed several for him in my apartment.

Sometimes things don't turn out for the better but instead turn out for the best... Like when we got a Pug instead of a mini dachshund, and decided to sell the house in Front Royal, VA, and settle down in Chapel Hill, NC... Best decisions ever.

I think the Trump Kool-Aid is laced with LSD... A powerful hallucinogenic, as I recall. :)

Autocracy, then, is where we're headed, I guess... Terrifying stupidity when you listen to anyone trying to say why Trump is the better choice for our country... Shit for brains... WTF...

Even though we may know the truth of it all, it doesn't stop us from grieving. Sad but true. As much as I'm trying to move forward, it's impossible not to remember the past... So hard, but I continue without them as it's my only option.

We're not meant to understand why, but to go and grow through it, as challenging as it is sometimes. To the bone sorrow is painful... My nerves are shot, as it's all taken a toll and has me nervous in the service... "Be still and know God is always here." I dreamt of Ruth and Papa, and I apologized to them both... as I felt I needed their forgiveness... Maybe we all seek forgiveness for our mistakes and our sins. We're only human... All too frail and vulnerable.

Be prepared because IF Trump wins the Election, he saves himself and sends the rest of us to deal with his mess.

"We're doomed," as Ruth used to like to say. Indeed.

My awareness is that she's alive and well in the afterlife and in good company as well... We all go there eventually and celebrate Life together again.

Trauma is Trauma & closure is by choice, I think, and happiness should come naturally... I would know, as I used to be.

I saw Ruth happy more often than not and remember her in Ireland in a pub with an old man who fell head over heels for her... Smitten, and she loved every moment of it. "Oh, he'll be fine she told him, when he asked if I minded it all? ... No worries, as I let her enjoy his fancy... It was a special moment, and I'm glad she enjoyed it.

"UNFIT for DUTY." ... and the 1st time I see this stated so clearly. Trump's New Slogan will be "PARDON ME." Sad but true as it's really why he's running and so desperate to win.

"A single cell organism" is how one European diplomat called Trump, whose only concern is for himself… He's like an A-Me-Bah at friend added… "An A-Meeee-Bah."

3/5/2024 and 47 years since our Papa left us… He was a man trying his best with a Herculean Effort every day of his life, right up to the end, coming back from mailing something he'd hoped might make a difference… We never knew what was so important… He lost control on some ice, and it ended my 23 years with the man. We honor his memory still to this day.

I'm trying and hoping to meet someone special, as I'm looking for more in a relationship than most men ever do… "Try again." I heard my angel whisper when Ruth's Personal Ad caught my attention… "Come & Go with me," she wrote… and the rest is history / her-story as well.

"Always look on the Bright Side of life."- Monte Python, a friend reminded me.

When on Tour with my parents in Israel, we visited a diamond factory where Papa bought Mum a beautiful ring… A lovely moment that everyone in our little group appreciated as being such a spontaneous gesture of their true love.

I recently saw a movie titled Perfect Days… "Not yet is not yet and Now is Now." was a conclusion a Japanese man said to his niece who'd run away from home… The two of them shared his workday cleaning Public Restrooms… He was able to find and share his peace with her. See it IF ever you can. He's beautiful.

"Less is more." More or less, I suppose… Be free from now on and let go of the rice in your hand, so as to free your hand from the trap… A jar set to catch monkeys as they refuse to let go.

McConnell gave Trump his testicles as a going-away gift as he's finally decided to retire. What a Chicken-Shit politician he turned into.

Biden's State of the Union Speech went well… Very well in fact… But people tend to forget so quickly, so we shall see IF indeed it does anything for him come voting time in November. But the Commander in Chief rose to the occasion for sure. House Leader Johnson looked like a complete fool in the background, with his stubborn mindset of stupidity… "The Art of The Squeal" is coming, I fear… But the fact that Trump is such an idiot has been declassified for all to see… Loud and Clear.

I witness Miracles of Love almost every day and feel truly blessed.

I miss not having an animal in my life... Bogie was such a presence for the almost 15 years he was with me... Pugs are awesome.

"Get on the path and Stay on the path."- as I make myself a protein shake and see Ruth's words to me to be "Strong & Courageous." ... I try to remain positive.

I recently saw Zone of Interest about a German family's experience living next to the Auschwitz concentration camp, trying to act like a normal family... Too hard to imagine all those poor souls going to their death... Barooch Ha Shem 6 million times is all I can say... 6 million times!!

"STOP framing it as Patriotism."- John Steward so eloquently stated to his listeners... It's bizarre and un-American and in fact Treasonous... "Demo-Crazy."- is my 2 cents.

I noticed a small strip mall near me where my go-to Chinese restaurant is no more... along with a Bowling Alley and Amonte's Pizza and an Allstate office as well have all closed their doors, as rents are just too high... A sign of the times.

IF closure is by choice, why isn't happiness as well? ... I'm not happy these days... Oh well, life goes on, happy or sad... It's good to know one's mental state in any case.

"Symbols help us remember what was dear to us once upon a time... Like Aladdin's Lamp, we can rub them slowly and relive a moment together."- *The Book of Awakening* by Mark Nepo, and my Miracle of Love, as my mom's business name was in fact Aladdin's...

My Totem Pole of how it all began with Ruth in Old Mystic, CT, in 2000, and the best Lobster Rolls ever, along with so many good memories.

I saw ONE LIFE with Anthony Hopkins and questioned how people's strength and endurance prevail in some situations like WW2? ... Compassion and commitment to the nth degree... He played the role almost too well and carried the spirit of all those he'd helped save.

"Pray More, worry less." I recently noticed on a woman's

T-shirt... God is omnipresent and always here, near and dear... Good reminder... Lighten up and don't take yourself so seriously.

St. Patrick's Day 3/17/2024 and my parents' wedding anniversary in 1953... I was there as their miracle of love as she was with child at the time... and he loved her so that he married her anyway, knowing the baby in her belly wasn't his… and that baby was me… I found a lovely and colorful picture of a bridge that day as my sign from above… Yet another bridge… Got to love it… "Don't ya know."- as Ruth used to like saying… "Don't ya know." … Indeed.

I'm questioning Trump's Bloodbath comment as selling sneakers and Bibles won't be enough to ever be granted forgiveness… A 2nd term would be a Death Sentence for democracy and sanity as we know it… Pretty scary.

"Let the sun shine, let the sunshine in… The Son shine in."- Me

"Incomparable-Imperfections" and Margin of Error… along with The Path of Least Resistance… as all are deeply thought-provoking, I think… IDK… To ponder.

"That's just the way it is."- Bruce Hornsby … Life's about changing, nothing ever stays the same."- Carol King … "I'm looking at the man in the mirror… I'm asking him to make a change."- Michael Jackson … "It's getting better all the time… Better, Better, B e t t e r… Getting so much better all of the time."- The Beatles … All help me to seek peace, as it still hurts.

On 3/22/24, I said goodbye to an old friend who said, "No more Trump jokes, please…" "Trump went to a proctologist because he's shitting bricks."- My final joke to him may have done it, as clearly he's pro-Trump… Poor Bastard, as he's not stupid but just doesn't get it, I guess.

"You can fool some of the people all of the time and all of the people some of the time… But you can't fool all the people all the time."- Bob Dylan

On 11/22/2021, Ruth asked me to take a picture of her, exactly 22 years to the day and to the hour of when we first met back in 11/22/1999 … I'm not sure why, but her departure from this world exactly two months later was predetermined in a way and a sign from above, as the universe knew… IT knew.

I think I'll always miss her, and I'm so grateful for the many Miracles of Love she has shared with me since her death…

A broken heart is broken and damaged forever, I think… "She's giving me a heart attack."- A line from a song years ago. My heart is broken for sure, and I may never recover the loss.

It's time to let go and let God … Divine Intervention might save us all at some point.

"I want you all to know that I love you and think about you all every day, as I keep you in my prayers, each and every day." I texted my siblings recently.

"You're tougher than a boiled owl."- I heard someone say during their negotiations… A great line.

They say that Time waits for no one, and yet what we fail to realize is that we have all the time in the world… An Eternity actually, to figure it all out… as we're born again, and again, and again… Makes the most sense, I think.

April showers, and I'm reminded of how much I enjoy a good Thunder and Lightning storm.

Be receptive and attentive to His Presence… and Gifts… Amazing Grace is always unfolding before our very eyes. "Don't become a Vegetable-Lasagna… Feed your brain."- My words to my brother… and a term Elaine on Seinfeld coined.

On April 1st, 2000, I'll always remember Ruth sharing the fact that we were engaged with her parents, and I appreciated her dad's joy and her mom's dismay… She couldn't hide it… and never did for the next 22 years that followed… Her loss, as what we shared was truly blessed, with or without her blessings… We both knew IT to be true and it was all that mattered.

Can you imagine The Crucifixion… We're asked to do just that every Easter… as He died on The Cross for us all, at the age of 33… BC / AD !!… Thank you, Jesus. Amen & Amen.

There are 4 words for you to remember and ponder… "I Trust You Jesus." … Say it to yourself throughout your day… It's Mana… Spiritual Light… We celebrate the fact that Christ has risen and is our connection to God the Father… "Praise God" is the most powerful prayer there is.

The fact is that more than 2000 years later, we still look back and remember His sacrifice… "Thank You Jesus."

Although we all struggle with our own day-to-day unique lives and their many challenges… We all fight the good fight.

"PERFECT," was my neighbor's response to my gift to her and my miracle of love on Easter Sunday.

Sometimes it takes so little and means so much to share kindness with someone simply.

A Magical Mystery Tour is how I describe my time with Monte and Ruth and Bogie and Mum… So awesome, from beginning to end… Until we meet again.

"You're a man of fewer and fewer words," I told my brother about my frustration with him and his unwillingness to keep reading something to feed his brain… "Help me help you," I said, but got no reaction… Parkinson's is an awful disease.

I am self-conscious and experiencing mild panic attacks over ever being intimate with someone other than Ruth in the future. In time, maybe, one day. It appears that we are witnessing real madness unfold in both Trump and Putin, as neither one is sane at this point… Sad and painful to watch… Evil and deranged.

Judge to Trump, "Bring your toothbrush," and if Republicans want to name something after him, they should make it a Federal Prison, a judge commented.

4/4/2024 and to be present in the present is the gift… and my last will & testament is done… A good thing, as "We're going to the end of the line."- The Traveling Willburys (So good in their day.)

Miscellaneous Loose Ends… To ponder… What? … All of it may be… To ponder IT All!!

"Don't it always seem to go that you don't know what you got till it's gone… they paved Paradise, and put up a Parking Lot."- Joni Mitchell.

Asfalt City… A movie with Shaun Pen about EMT workers in NYC… Maybe we need to see the other side? … The crazy side…

"A Crackpot with power is really dangerous."- Liz Chaney.

He's gone from being a sick pup to being a Sick-Fuck- My words.

I saw DOGMAN recently and enjoyed this bizarre story, but told really well… MonkeyMan as well…

After 6 months of captivity, "Hope is mandatory," and so eloquently expressed by the families of those still held hostage in Gaza by Hamas.

"Life, Liberty, and The Pursuit of Happiness… and where I met Emily Poe back in 1987" … I give thanks every morning.

I'm on a mission from God, to find joy in my life once again… New Beginnings.

4/8/2024 and a Solar Eclipse… Won't happen again for 20 years.

Take your inner voice seriously… Keep your "I" open and feel His Presence… Omnipresence/ Omnipotence, if you can imagine.

"I think, therefore I am."- René Descartes, the father of philosophy… Hmmm?… Makes me think… "I am, therefore I think."- AI… It's here.

"After changes upon changes, we are more or less the same… After changes, we are more or less the same."- CSNY… 50+ years ago… Crosby, Stills, Nash & Young at Woodstock.

To Life… Not easy, but so be it… Pace yourself is my best advice.

Sometimes, we don't see what's right in front of us… What do you see? … Who do you see? … Stop, Look & Listen !!…

When we lose hope, we lose everything… So, I try to rekindle hope in both of my brothers' lives, as well as my own.

I wrote "Wait for it… Wait for it." as my reconstruction period, and "Said & Done" as my Renaissance… I had to write it all down… Taking Note is how I write… Making note of it all one day at a time.

I choose to practice God's presence versus the presence of any problems.

There is abundant life in God's presence … I need to live more fully in the life I've been given.

Our time here is temporary and goes by too quickly… Only 24 hours in a day for a reason, as we bear the weight of it all just one day at a time.

I walked past a mother and daughter who were probably 4 or 5, and she gave me such a beautiful smile… I thought that IF my sister had a daughter, what an amazing young woman she'd be.

When I shared this with her, she told me that I made her day.

I think it's poetic justice that a woman will indeed be Trump's downfall.

I recently saw CIVIL WAR and hope it never happens for real… Anything seems possible, though.

4/13/2024 and Iran launches Drones towards Israel… All were intercepted… Drones over NJ … Germany's Government has collapsed along with France… Trump is about to take control as our President, with Vance being next in line… WTF… IDK anymore… Cartoon Characters in Toon-Town… "God help us."

Ultimately, from beginning to end, it's all good… Occasional Speed Bumps are simply a part of it all, but that's life. Shit gets real now and then… We roll with it, baby.

I try to put on a happy face, but it still hurts and makes me feel sad… I'm determined to be at peace with it eventually. Time takes time. Hard to believe 3 years on 1/23/2025, and indeed "Time is the unreal reflection of Eternity," and all I can say… Time out then maybe… Time out.

My awareness is that it ended in such an awful and unbelievable way that will forever be so hard to accept and move forward from… I was there and couldn't believe what I was seeing… Beyond belief… She ended it the way she did and left me to pick up all the bits and pieces, including her, when I cut her down and tried to breathe life back into her dead body… I had to try. I had to. I survived the worst possible ending ever and will always wonder why she did it?… But life goes on… My life here, and hers there.

Some questions have no acceptable answers, and we're left to fill in the blanks as best we can. She is responsible for this outcome, and maybe it can be a source of strength since it was so tragic, and you have moved your life beyond it. The scars will always be there. - Glenn Simon told me, and it speaks volumes. "Yes, indeed, we bear the scars we've been dealt," I replied, grateful for his words. Some speed bumps are bigger than others, I guess, and require us to slow our roll. I've been forced to do exactly that—to slow my roll and proceed with caution.

I did somehow befriend a lovely, gentle man a couple of years ago by the name of Bill Ross… My Mr. Bill… a very spiritual Black man who loves Mexican food as much as I do, along with talking politics and cars… He makes me smile and laugh out loud and insists on taking our picture after we've voted, hoping that documenting it might sway things in our favor… Not so this last time when we witnessed the unimaginable happen with Trump's re-election… "WTF happened!?" we exclaimed. Anyway, he's become a good buddy and I'm blessed to have found him.

My life sometimes feels like an episode of The Twilight Zone or The Outer Limits… I never could tell the difference as they were both so well done… Another little something Bill and I share.

I survived my greatest fear, and she did not… Mine was losing her and hers was losing her mind… The chemo broke her, and she'd made up her mind to exit Stage Left… Stubborn to the end… My comfort is that she's alive and well, exploring her past with her relatives and mine in her spiritual quest in the After Life… As we will all get to do one day when our life ends… Sooner or later.

We are given life, but it's a temporary gift and one that we eventually lose… Until we discover Eternal life, and I believe we are eternal spirit beings along for the ride.

"Walk / Walk / Walk."- The crosswalk machine squeaks, as I wait for permission to cross… It always makes me smile.

"I'm walkin' here / I'm walkin' here."- Dustin Hofmann in Midnight Cowboy, as he spontaneously added to his script… Genius… "I'm walkin' here… I'm walkin' here, as are we all.

I've said all I can, trying to see my life from a new and improved perspective… I'm done, Said & Done… as I'm past My Best if served by Expiration Date… Thanks for listening.

TBC… "To Be Continued." … It's life after all, and we keep on keeping on… Onward Christian Soldier… NEXT!!

Bogie & me… Best dog ever.

TBC...TO BE CONTINUED.

Ruth used to say TBC every now and then... "To be continued."

The here and now... My brother shared a story of how, after our Papa had passed in a car accident on 3/5/1977, he had an experience of walking with him through the woods, until they came to a fork ... "This is where we part... he said, but we'll see each other again one day."

I believe life begins when we say "I love you" to someone... Say it to someone today if you can... It changes everything.

We all try our best not to disappoint and to make a difference... and in the end, our Report Card of Life will reflect that, I believe. We did our best. My pain was deep... So deep that it compelled me to explore the very depths of my soul, alone... All alone, as we all truly are. The painting of the Blue Heron on the side of the SC Aquarium was a premonition of how Ruth would appear to me after her death. It still happens now and then, as a demonstration of her continued life beyond this one. The blue heron has become my favorite bird, but all of them are wonderful to watch and appreciate.

"You either trust or you don't... You either have faith or you don't... You either believe or you don't."- My words.

The 2 1/2-year anniversary of Ruth's death was on 7/23/2024 and was also my dad's birthday anniversary, as he would have been 101, as was our mom when she passed on 5/23/2023 ... Ruth passed on 1/23/2022 and we question what is it about the number 23?... Too many deaths in my family seem to occur on the 23rd for some reason. Monte as well.

My story continues, and I write because it helps ... My 4 journals are "A Real Piece of Work... My 68 years on planet earth," as my Autobiography, then "Wait for it...Wait for it," as my last 2 years after Ruth's death... Followed then with "Said and Done," as my reconstruction and renaissance period, and my Herculean Effort to keep on keeping on at this point... and TBC being my 4th and final chapter of my story, for now anyway. I'm ready to write a new chapter with a new leading lady, maybe... We'll see.

I survived what I never imagined I could as her suicide broke me. I've had many wonderful demonstrations and miracles of love of her continued presence and love, it is undeniable at this point that life does indeed continue in the afterlife, and it's a profound blessing to be aware of this as a fact of life.

"Stay alive, I will find you." - Ruth would sometimes say, quoting a great line from a movie she loved, which I think involved a Cruise Ship flipping upside-down, if I remember correctly. Anyway, her loving spirit self is alive and well. No doubt, and she wants me to find joy with someone new. It's not easy as I'm still healing from it all. I'm too sensitive and have always worn my heart on my sleeve for all to see… My Achilles' Heel… and it is what it is, and I can't change that. Not sure if I want to.

"Approach My Throne of Grace with bold confidence, receiving My Peace with a thankful heart."- *The Book of Awakening by Mark Nepo* and my Life-Saver, gifted to me by my best friend Monte's wife, Anna Sugarman... I'm not sure if I'd still be here had she not shared it with me. A daily read of just one page a day, and like having a moment with one's guardian angel. Get a copy and read it with a yellow marker, as you'll find wisdom in almost every paragraph… Feed your heart and your soul each and every day… "Ruach" = Wind in Hebrew, and also means Spirit as well.

Like intermittent windshield wipers, we must allow it to decide when to wipe… It knows when it's time, so let go and let God. - My spiritual 2 cents.

"Acceptance and Adjustments" are key elements in life…

"I'm proud of you," May Su told me recently.

My day ended with a video confirmation that life continues after death, and yet another Miracle of Love to ponder and give thanks for. My brother Sandy and I are each other's sherpa and shaman these days, and I told him that I'm his Navy SEAL partner who will dive after him if need be. "That's the power of love," Huey Louis reminds us, while wearing his sunglasses.

Ruth graduated from The School of Hard Knocks… Life ain't always easy and smooth sailing… We all cope the best we can, until we can't anymore. She'd made her decision to exit Stage Left, leaving our Bogie on our bed, and it was for me to find her hanging in our master closet… I could feel her spirit self watching me go into action in an attempt to save her… but it was too little too late. Although I got her breathing again, her spirit had moved on. I felt her watching me with her guardian angel as I did my best to deal with it all, by myself, from now on.

Passover was on 4/22/2022, and I'm aware that it's one thing to celebrate and honor a holiday because the calendar reminds us to, and quite another to honor each day as a holy day because we feel God's Presence in our life... Omnipresent and Omnipotent.

My daily regimen includes Kodiak pancakes with granola and walnuts, a multivitamin, a Fatty omega supplement, a Grape Seed Extract, a Turmeric Supplement, a Potassium pill, and some Collagen Peptides as part of my healthy routine. My meds include a Statin for cholesterol, a Blood Pressure pill, and an Antidepressant to calm the nerves. Not bad, my sister told me as I'm 71 and getting older... I believe Prevention is the best medicine... Can't hurt.

It's always darkest before the dawn, and The Day the music stopped on 10/7/2023 is a new Interactive Experience telling the story of the Hamas attack killing 1500 innocent participants that day... WAR is declared and the Middle East is in chaos ... It's horrible to watch, and the world is aware and saddened by it all. Too many more innocent victims are caught in the crossfire... Too many children and babies.

On 4/24/2024, I missed my exit coming back from an audiologist apt. and ended up on Airport Rd. going towards Chapel Hill... I stopped to grab a slice of Pizza and felt moved to go to the UNC Hospital traffic circle, where I'd dropped Ruth off for the last time on 1/7/2022 ... I felt her with me as I spotted an Electric Storm Blue RAV4 letting me know she was indeed there with me ... We both enjoyed the slice remembering us going to the Museum of Natural History and The Planetarium in NYC and getting a slice before entering. The next day's reading shared that "Memories are not images of loved ones returning to us, but are in fact the spirits of loved ones visiting us." ... I was speechless and humbled and had to share this with my friend May Su who said "Welcome them...Enjoy them...Treasure them." Her words of wisdom to me... IT didn't end the way I thought it would but IT didn't begin the way I thought it would either... Blessed from beginning to end in a way. I have to accept it all. No choice really. "We do what we must do and we do it well."... She gave it her all, until she just couldn't anymore.

Trump's Trials and Tribulations increase exponentially as his true ways are all exposed at this point. "Make America Regret Again."- My quote, and my question is, do you think Trump will bring back the Guillotine... and tell us all to Eat Cake? … He'll shred the Constitution, I heard one news person say. The terrifying fact is that a majority of Americans actually wanted him to be elected … They want a Dictatorship, and it's just so bizarre to understand… The world, for now, has gone mad.

I feel like I've been gifted a 2nd chance at life and love. I'll take it and see what happens… Give Peace a Chance and love as well… I pray on it every day, and for my family and the world, and that somehow God's Will must indeed unfold within the chaos of it all. "For Thine is the Kingdom and the Power and the Glory for ever and ever." AMEN and AMEN. Acceptance and adjustments are key elements in life. "Proud of you," May Su told me recently. She's a wise old soul, and I'm glad she's still there for me.

What have you got to lose? … Be the lion. Have the courage to move forward without them… Ruth wants me to keep going.

"I have me an annuity, but I need cash now," and may be the best commercial jingle ever in my opinion. Call J.G. Wentworth … 877 CASH NOW !!… I remember sharing it with my sister, and we all joined in to sing it while laughing together. The Schaefers love to laugh whenever we get together. It helps us heal, I think, as pain in life is unavoidable… We all dodge bullets at times. Duck Donald Duck. I can't help but wish he had been taken out that day.

We, the People, doesn't mean the ".1%" … The wealthy do not understand us or reality, and we now live in The Twilight Zone and The Outer Limits, as the craziest people are now in charge.

Sometimes life grabs you by the short hairs and doesn't let go, just to mess with us and remind us who's really in charge. Germany's Government has collapsed. What's next?… Not good.

Today's paradigm shift might be just what we've been hoping for. Let's be open to it and grateful for it, as it might change everything. I think we're all ready for something good to take place for a change.

Is there a question you would ask me? … What? … Ask me then? … "What a journey life is."- our Sandy shared recently, and the understatement for the day.

"I am so Glad that I have been fortunate enough to have my Shirpa (You) with me… all the time."- Sandy's words to me.

I think we're both each other's Shirpa at this point. We both just needed a friend in our lives… Someone to lean on and laugh with.

Ruth came to me as a Blue Heron on Feb.1st, 2022 … "2/1/2022" a week after she'd passed, and I'll always appreciate how this magnificent creature allowed me to get closer than ever before. It was her, no doubt… "Life never ends, but only changes."- David Bowie … God is Good.

"The world in all its mystery and difficulties cannot be improved upon, only experienced."- A lesson of Taoism.

"Exceptionally wonderful."- Sir Paul McCartney, and so beautifully stated in describing his time with The Beatles… "Exceptionally wonderful" is how I choose to remember all those who have passed, knowing that we'll see them all again one day, when it's our turn to exit stage left.

"I got 2 or 3 dozen Condolence Cards after Ruth passed, and I only kept the 1st and the last one I got… May Su's was last… Her wise words and kindness were of enormous help. The Holidays are still tough without them and although I no longer grieve, I do miss what we once shared… and why I find it hard to be with her I told her… as she reminds me of Ruth, and her love and appreciation of both her and Tai Chi… and why I had to delay getting together with her until next year as it's still too painful a reminder of what once was but is no more… I hope she understands. … Enjoy your holiday, I said, and thanks again for everything."- My words to May Su, along with an apology.

I sent Sandy Papas' menorah, as per his wishes shared with me in my sleep. Papa last communicated with me when he asked that his scarf be placed with Mum before her funeral, and I told Nic just that… He was pleased, and I feel his same delight now knowing Sandy has his silver menorah in his collection.

A Hanukkah miracle, as this year it falls on Christmas Day 2024. We both believe it's at least a hundred years old… Could be.

I can't help but think the entire world is about to experience a Brutal change for the worse. Much worse, maybe. I hope I'm wrong… Let us pray for Divine Intervention at this point.

"Turn and face the change… Cha-Cha-Cha-Changes."- David Bowie … "Nothing ever stays the same… You're gonna be a better man." … and "Time may change me, but I can't change time." … He was a great artist in addition to his musical contributions.

What else can I say but that we've been here before and we'll be here again, as Spirit Beings we are born again and again and again... I hope you agree, and appreciate that love is the only thing we get to take with us when we go... So love all you can... Love !!...

My book is done, and as my Herculean Effort, I'm pleased with how it turned out. I wonder how my story will actually end one day... Hmmm? ... IDK... and "There in lies the beauty of Life." Trust in Ha Shem... My brother, Sandy, and another wise old soul told me.

All mine... I've done an exhibition or two.

MY POEM AND PREMONITION.

When I finished writing my first book/journal, as my Autobiography, I'd thought I was done writing… It turned out to be just the beginning, and three years later, I think it's done… We shall see… IDK… I just don't know.

I shared my news with a few friends and family members, and May Su answered by saying:

Hi Phil,

"Very Interesting Perspectives" … V.I.P.… What a unique title for your book.

I am incredibly proud of you for all that you have accomplished.

Now you can sit back and savor your efforts.

Happy memories.

This was my poem to Ruth once upon a time… I think we were both so moved by it.

Titled: **"EVERYWHERE I GO."**

You are my second wind. My mind set a spin

My reincarnation

My redemption,

My every whim

My breath of fresh air… My very spirit within

You know who you are… And now know that it is "I" who loves you more than you'll ever know.

Spend eternity with me… Won't you?

We'll build our mansion in the sky

And live happily ever after

"You" … Make me smile

Inside and out,

I love you so.

She knew our love would be forever and eternal, as her wind chime declared after her passing… Got to love it… We shared something special, and I will love her forever.

"THANK YOU, RUTH."

P.S. Until we meet again.

Ruth and I used to walk around a small lake behind our townhouse in Governors Village, and we'd stop at a wooden bridge to say a prayer for someone who'd recently passed.

I went there on 12/24/2024 to make a prayer for her, as it's been about three years since she passed… I told her that if she needs to transition to her next plane, that it's okay, and I want her to… Go, then, I said, and we'll reconnect later… A Golden Retriever came to me and gave me kisses, so I knew she was there, as Ruth had owned a Golden Retriever when we first met, and it was so very meaningful… His name was Sam, and he was another good dog.

At 71, I'm looking back on it all, remembering as much as I can, as it won't ever be the same without them… The Circle of Life… Amazing while it lasted… Simply Amazing really… Pure & simple.

My final words of advice would be that as human beings, we are resilient beyond anything we can imagine… Seek the truth and by doing so, we change… It's life… Enjoy as much as you can. XOXO

"When you can't, you must … And when you must, you can." Anonymous.

© Copyright Phil Schaefer 2024

"Peace…Health…Love."

LOOSE ENDS & SCREWS...

"Blackbird singing in the dead of night... Take these broken wings and learn to fly... All your life... You were only waiting for this moment to arise..." – Blackbird by The Beatles.

I miss Monte, my best friend for almost 50 years... I remember driving to NYC with him to see where John Lennon was killed... Our loss was profound... "Imagine there's no heaven, I wonder if you can?" ... He's probably laughing as he knows the truth... Imagine Heaven exists... I wonder if you can?

Stop The Squeal. "We choose freedom."- Kamala Harris, and what a breath of fresh air... Much needed at the time, as Trump is just crazy... Bat Shit Crazy!

"Au Revoir mon amour, a biento."- A commercial on TV that makes me smile whenever it plays... Too funny.

"So, what's your Super Power? Parallel-Parking?" - Deadpool

"We survive the storms and open ourselves to actual adaptability and even balance when we look up and see blue sky above."- *The Book of Awakening* by Mark Nepo.

I'm reading it again, every day... for the 3rd time.

Trump calls Harris a "low-I.Q. person" and in so doing reveals his No I.Q. state of mind... He's one disturbed individual.

"We are not going back."- Kamala reminds us, but it turned out to be too little too late as the majority voted for Trump by a slim margin... WTF people? ... Is the blind now leading the blind?

WARNING... The DOJ warns us in regards to a 2nd Trump term... "Danger... Danger Will Robinson."- Lost in Space... as we have now entered the Darker Ages in our History... He's a Dick-Tater.

I've had too many out-of-body moments along with so many demonstrations or miracles of love in my life at this point, and I know that we are spirit beings having human experiences and life never really ends... Not easy being me or you or any of us, as our lives have unfolded over the years and we're where we're meant to be at this moment... "Don't confuse me with facts." Our Papa used to say to us.

Try not to judge what you don't fully understand... Empathy.

Ruth introduced me to Roller Coasters, and if ever you can try sitting in the front car… It's both the scariest and smoothest place to be… It's life.

We shared a moment of mutual appreciation as a family and something we haven't done in a while… Each of us is trying our best to just survive… No one has an easy life… Our family gatherings are rare, but they are powerful.

It never ceases to amaze me and may just be a maze we're expected to traverse until we reach the end, like a house of mirrors… We don't know where the end is until we get there. Papa and I once did a maze together when I was 5 or 6 years old… a baby and so young, but I remember… A good lesson.

If you didn't know how old you are, how old would you be? … Who were you in a past life? … To ponder.

I never meant to hurt or insult or cause irreparable damage between us … I'm sorry if I have done just that… I still hold our friendship dear… Some things are beyond our control… If you'd prefer not to continue, I understand completely… I'm sorry if I offend every now and then… It's not intentional… I just lost my better half, is all, and coping without them is unfamiliar to me… It's like needing crutches but not having any, and so I stumble.

"Let my love open the door… to your heart." … Trust… and today's demonstration… I look for Miracles of Love every day.

I'm aware of my appreciation of simple silence… Quiet!…

So pure and simple… Be quiet… It's profound and peaceful… Very Zen and easy… A quiet meditation… Shhhhh… Shh!!

Perfection doesn't exist, except in heaven maybe… Of course.

We must be patient… and persistent and courageous as well… "Good job, Mr. Schaefer," Ruth used to tell me.

V.I.P. or Very Interesting Perspectives… is my book… as I'm willing and able to bare my soul… It's hard to do, but it's important if you think about it… Could you, if asked to?

My journals are:

"A Real Piece of Work… My 68 years on planet earth." + "WAIT FOR IT… WAIT FOR IT." + "Said & Done." along with "TBC… To be continued." and now "Loose Ends & Screws…" I had more to say, I guess…

I simply make a note to publish one day, maybe… My Herculean Effort is to restore a semblance of normalcy to my life… No small doing.

I don't wish to be judged or criticized or weighed or measured …

IF you need to do that, may I suggest you look in the mirror… Have fun and let me know when you're done… Life is too short and we all do the best we can… I'm sorry if I disappoint.

How connected our pallet is to our memories… In our case, the raw dough of her croissants, the Crock-Messier and her crepes… her chickens and chicken liver dishes… and her mandabutchnic (Potato Bread), all make for our special shared gourmet flavors and unique to our family tree of experiences… So good.

"I'm not always my best company."- My brother shared with me recently… He's not alone.

"Put a woman in charge." - A music video, and so powerful.

"Life can be a real shit-show at times."- My words…

I'm sure I'm not the only one who thinks so… Sad but true.

I'm aware that Ruth got my iPhone exactly 5 years ago in July of 2020, and the 1st pic she took was her smiling face… My miracle of love, as I remember her, never wanting to be a burden on any of us, and a vow she'd made with herself… Stubborn to the end… The End… "I've eaten enough," she told me when I offered to make her breakfast that morning… It didn't register as it should have warned me, but I let it go.

You are blessed… Appreciate all that you have… It's a Christmas Miracle… Just look around, I told a friend who didn't know what to be thankful for… So much, really, I pointed out.

Kamala Harris might just be our new knight in shining armor… as Trump struggles to make sense of anything these days… Cloud 9 going to 10… He's one sick fuck if you ask me.

I feel like a new and improved me needs to be, starting now.

"Thank You Phil" was her message to me exactly a month after she'd passed… On 2/22/2022, nine images appeared on TV, all with the same message… "Thank You Phil." with the last one having a small heart dotting the "i" … 2/22/2022… I love it.

I just don't know? … What will be will be… Why am I still being faithful to her? … It's been three years… My mission is to find joy in my life once again… IF possible… I sometimes doubt it.

For things to change, we must change… And so it goes, and so we grow… Grow then!!

I've always appreciated Maya Angelou and her wisdom…" IF you come to make a difference, you laugh as often as possible." and "I don't trust a person who doesn't love themselves." - Wow!! And "Be careful when a naked person offers you a shirt."

The Scarecrow Award… It honors those who are outstanding in their field."- Glen Simon shared once… He's out standing in his field… I've known him for about 30 years.

50 years ago, Nixon resigned. I was traveling in England, and a bartender asked us what we thought about it. … It was the first time we'd heard of it, and we were shocked to say the least… Tricky-Dick.

I will continue to ponder it all… Grateful and optimistic for whatever comes my way… I thank God Almighty… The Kingdom and The Power and The Glory forever and ever.

Mission Possible… Be your best self… Find your Joi de vie… It's out there somewhere… You're getting close to your next destination in life… It's coming soon.

"V.I.P. => Very Interesting Perspectives." But my story continues, one day at a time… Slow but sure… Peace, Health, Love, and Hope are all part of my morning prayer.

"Verbal Flagelance" is how I'd describe Trump's thoughts on anything at this point… One big Gas Leak… A fart in the wind.

Walz was the 1st to call Trump weird, asking who mentions Hannibal Lector or Sharks in the water… Also asking why we've never seen Trump laugh in 6 years?… He tells it like it is.

Be debrouyar… Be resourceful… Be kind to others and to yourself as well… Being is important, being important is not … We simply try our best every day… It's what we do… All of us, every day… Keep praising G-D… and Keep on keeping on !!

Sometimes when everything hurts, persistence pays… Keep trying… Try again… You got this… Make it work.

"Make it so."- Jean Luke Picard on Star Trek.

Breaking News… Trump sees a Proctologist because he's Shitting Bricks, and Vance reveals just how stupid he really is… Shit for brains… Both one and the same.

"Crime was up during the Trump years, and that's not including the crimes he committed."- Walz ... "Wall to Walz coverage." MSNBC is very clever.

"Winning isn't for everyone."- An Olympic message to be appreciated as a commercial shared.

Have you never experienced a moment of what might have been, had you only just taken action?... A missed opportunity is just that... Gone forever... The Power of Now, as the present moment, is the gift.

"IF it's going to be, it's up to me."- Anonymous.

"Believing is Seeing."- My conclusion.

On 8/11/2024, Sandy's Ilene came to me in a dream, smiling from ear to ear and so happy... Communicating the importance of staying positive... I shared it with Sandy and his kids.

"You really had a wonderful life, George Bailey," Clarence, his guardian angel, tells him in A Wonderful Life.

"There's no salvation without sacrifice." - I forget who said this, but they hit the nail on the proverbial head, I think.

"To see takes time." - Georgia O'Keeffe... "We all need something to care for... We resist being pruned."

An epiphany isn't an epiphany until it's shared with someone and more fully appreciated.

"Be Strong & Courageous." - A message on a cup that Ruth left for me to find... I keep it on top of my refrigerator along with the last styrofoam cup she got me on our last Road Trip... She surprised me with a much-needed cup of coffee in a most unique cup that I just had to hold onto... It's a beautiful reminder.

"We are here to live out loud... To love out loud." - My realization.

Life sometimes demands that we do for ourselves... We shall see... All aboard The Trump Titanic... He's going down and he knows it... Not enough lifeboats... Every man for himself... He'll leave us all to fend for ourselves for sure.

"One small step for man ... One giant leap for mankind," and still such a profound quote.

I made a new friend and neighbor named Sandy with similar stories of loss and grieving... It's life... Her partner's name was Phil... Hmmm? ... I'm not sure if we're meant to be friends yet.

Allow your vulnerabilities to be seen… A semblance of normalcy would be nice… My goal and my true colors… The truth and nothing but The Truth, then.

Do you remember the cereal commercial and slogan "It's gonna be a great day." … Their Jingle… "They're Great!!" Frosted Flakes.

T.G.I.F. or "Think Greatness is Feasible." - My interpretation.

A paradigm shift… As it can now be said every day and not just on Friday… Might be my most powerful quote ever offered.

Sing Hallelujah. Come on, get happy, we're waiting for the judgement day…

"Pray more, worry less."- a T-shirt message I noticed while shopping, and another saying "Jesus loves you."

I got word that a publisher wants to publish my book… V.I.P. … Very Interesting Perspectives… and will include my 5 journals as one book.

Edit / Page Layout / Cover Design / Print / Promotion Mktg / Distribution/ Book-Signings / Sales / Next Stage of promotions… We shall see… IDK… Might be expensive?

Time for healing and seeing what lies ahead… Be open to it all… Anything can happen… and usually does.

Lord, point me in the direction You want me to go, and I will follow Your lead.

"You can lead a horse to water, but you can't make him drink … and you can lead someone to wisdom, but you can't make them think."- My words and conclusion as relating to anyone have become more and more difficult these days… It just is.

"There are 3 kinds of people… Folks who make things happen…

Folks who watch things happen… and Folks who ask what the heck just happened?" … Which one are you?

"Friendships either grow, or they go… I fear ours has gone." - My words to 3 friends who are no more… Alas…

"Thanks for the memories."- Bob Hope … and "Reality, what a concept." - Robin Williams and "No Reservations."- Anthony Bourdain … All so Powerful in their contributions.

I have alienated almost everyone I know since she passed. What ya gonna do?… They're doing as well as mine, I think.

The Chinese say, "Destiny is Destiny." ... They also say, "May you live in interesting times." ... Could be good or could be bad? ... We're asked to wait and see... The Chaos of it all is life itself.

"Think Big but act small, as we're both humbled and grateful for everything God gives us." - My awareness... Rest in the shadow of His Presence... and try not to lift over 3 tons today, I told my brother once, as he often finds himself as a one-man crew.

"Look at you." - Ruth would say to me sometimes ... and I hear her whisper to me now and then... "We're gettin' there."- her words as well... "YOU" ... and "You'll live." along with "Hello Stranger."- She had a unique take on it all and was very smart.

It's hard to sweep 23 years of memories under the rug. Impossible really... I apologize if my shared miracles of love are perhaps too intimate and too much at times... My bad.

Time to get serious about my health... F.H.B. for real... (Family Hold Back) ... Make good choices... Metabolism killers make it harder.

Emanuel... G-D is with us... Yahweh

Let's make Empathy our strength... Yeshua = Sent.... Jesus.

Celebrate the idea of a Re-Birth-Day... To actually be born again... Born anew... Again and again and again, maybe even.

"You kept us breathing in a world without air." - An Israeli father's words at the UN once... Soon after Hamas killed his son... Such cruelty... We all shared their loss.

"We need to keep on keeping on, until we are a united people of these United States." - Stevie Wonder. DNC... and so many great moments ..." Show some respect." and "Be Patriotic."

"We must put country 1st."- and "We are all in this together... For the people." - Kamala, and "America, we are not going back."

And "Hope is making a comeback." - Michelle Obama.

"While struggling with the pain of change, it is often impossible to see the new self we are becoming." Embrace it.

I've become a big believer in miracles and where there's hope, there's the potential for miracles... TRUST... My epiphany.

RFK Jr. = Really Fucking Knuts, as he's always been, I think.

Prepare for The Final Famine... Stock your pantry... China is buying up our Farm land... Along with Bill Gates... Fucking Sell-Out.

I witnessed a single vertical thread of bright light for a brief moment... as a reminder of a presence coming to say hello, and I saw a very slender young deer walk by.

Mum's funeral was the last time we all gathered together... She was there... No doubt about it.

"Escalation management" is a term I just heard in regard to the Middle East... Not Good... Not good at all.

The last week of summer with fall coming soon... Cool and hopefully engaging with someone new.

"If your mind were a suitcase and could only hold 5 things, what would they be?" - To ponder then... What's really most important to you? ... We witnessed our mother doing just this once when a forest fire suddenly happened... Frightening!!

We must keep on keeping on by doing whatever we need to do...

As Doing is indeed living... My writing has become My Doing...

"Living is a conversation with no end."- *The Book of Awakening* by Mark Nepo

School is back in session and includes the school of Hard Knocks... It's life... Watch out for Stress-Traps... as they latch on and don't let go easily... "Hold on tight... It's gonna be a bumpy ride."- Betty Davis ... Ilene smiled with my words that day we met... Sandy took us on a wild ride through the woods in his Nissan Pathfinder.

Go find your next great adventure... Where to and who with?

I don't know... Who then? ... Who?

"I'm going to Graceland... Heaven above... Where we will be received... We're going to Graceland."- Paul Simon, and one of my favorite songs and performers.

"A Big faux pas."- One great French expression to know.

"On the road again." - Our Mom and my miracle of love today as I left with her blessings... "Be confident every step of the way." ... Be patient with yourself as well... Remain calm.

CIE Tours... The best, and may just be what I'm still here for ...

Continued Intimate Experiences... I'll always remember Elizabeth and Bob as King and Queen of the castle... Their joy was through the roof... Along with his appreciation of Scones with butter... or should I say Butter with scones.

Acknowledge God's Presence, and pray His Will be done…

Every day in every way… Praise God every day, several times a day… "Barooch Ha Shem." … Amen and Amen.

Labor Day and "Thank you for your words today… We heard you… You were speaking from your heart." My words to Mark, my Sister's husband… Pretty huge actually.

Shit, shower, and shave… Shake a leg and start your day… Every day, really.

Lunch with Sandy, my neighbor, and a new friendship… Maybe?

"Seeing is no longer believing."- A commercial. re: AI stating the obvious… Pretty scary, really.

My life has become quite different without them … Their absence is greatly felt … I ain't lying… We're the ones left to suffer the loss… Sad-Cow-Syndrome, as I call it.

I'm going to pick myself up, brush myself off, and start all over again … One day at a time… Pace yourself.

"Like a fish turning water into air, we use our heart and our mind and our spirit as we must turn our experience into something that can sustain us… It means turning pain into wonder and heartache into joy." - My realization.

D-Day with a debate as Harris must now prove herself and Trump must show us his true colors… Let's pray for her.

Herstory in the making… You go, girl… "The most un-American candidate ever."- Scaramouch said on MSNBC re: Trump… She decapitated and castrated Trump in just one debate. "You're a disgrace," Kamala Harris told him to his face.

Do I continue to live in the past, telling my stories of once upon a time as if they're still relevant? … or is it water under the bridge… Are they still important … I think they are, but I may be the only one.

How does one recreate oneself when it feels like I've done it all?

9/11/2024 and a day to remember them all… God Bless. "The blue skies above remind us that our hearts haven't fully healed."- Lester Holt, NBC News… Well said, kind sir.

"Trump most influenced undecided voters, who have now in fact decided."- Jimmy Fallon.

We smile more often than not… The Schaefers.

Right here… Right now… Optimism… We're where we're meant to be… And ACTION!!

I'm aware that my apartment is my campsite and offers up some elbow room as well… My home away from home.

On Friday the 13th… I saw a movie, The Critic… and I made some good choices at Fresh Market… I also decided not to spend the day with Sandy as 4 to 5 hours with kids is too much right now… They're all strangers to me, and I think it strange that she invited me, and I had to cancel… Glad I did.

My vantage point has changed, and I must move forward from now on … Find a new partner… I pray on it daily.

"He cannot hold on to any coherent thinking."- Mary Trump … His niece, a psychologist… Speaks volumes.

"Turn each experience into something that sustains you and breathe." … "Y'are-de-tority."- a Scottish horseman meaning you are the authority… or you know what you're talking about, I heard two Scotsmen say to each other.

"People are ready for acts of civility."- Will Ferrell and … "We are all actors."- Marlyn Brando.

I'm not sure how much longer I'll be here, as I'll be 72 soon… Our own mortality? … Hmmm? … To ponder… We do what we must do and we do it well… At least we like to think so.

"We light an eternal flame in our hearts for the ones we've lost."

I remember being at Nic's house and having a conversation with our mum about food and table manners and forks and knives… She appreciated my appreciation of spoons, and got up and went over to a drawer in the kitchen, pulled out a large silver spoon, and gave it to me… I was happy to get it… A genuine and generous gift… I no longer have it as I lost it during my move…

But I remember, and I can still see it, and I still have it in my heart… I hope there's a Lost and Found in Heaven.

From Old Mystic Seaport, CT, to Kitty Hawk, NC … and so much in between… Alaska to Hawaii, Ireland to Scotland, Seattle, Chicago, Austin, New Orleans, Roslyn, NM, Sedona, AZ, and San Francisco too, Chapel Hill, Raleigh, Asheville, Boone, The Highlands, The Outer Banks,

So. Port SC, and all our camping and Hotels along the way… She gave a good tour… Great Tour.

I can, I will, and I must move forward as that's life… Be here now… Live your life… I said goodbye to another familiar face…

Changes… "Turn & face the change."- D. Bowie

Just the one… Me, myself & I… Table for three, then? … Yes, table for three… All three of me.

A sick day filled with crazy thoughts of penguins and octopus and extreme discomfort and more… A reaction to my Covid booster shot… Maybe?

G-D knows us better than we know ourselves… We must "Let go and Let G-D." … Think about it.

No more dreams and aspirations at this point, I'm afraid…

Life as I knew it is no more… Sad but true… Poke me with a fork,

I think I'm done… Salvage what you can and create something new with someone new, IF possible? … I'm not sure it is… What am I hoping for? … Love maybe? … I'm not happy anymore, and I'm terribly lonely as well… Painfully so.

My heart and spirit are broken beyond repair, I fear… with no Time Machine to press Rewind… The End is always near.

Walk into the future with your eyes closed and tell me what you see? … Can you see anything? … What then? … What? … Tell me.

I survived a rough week of being sick and am grateful to finally feel better, ready to move forward with meeting someone.

My epiphany is that my effort to resuscitate Ruth was not only to try to save her life, but to allow her spirit self to witness me doing so, as she always doubted my ability to rise to the occasion, IF ever it were necessary… IT was !!… She was gone.

I could feel her and her spirit guide watching me do what I knew I had to… She was pleasantly surprised and proud of me as well… "Good job, Mr. Schaefer," she used to tell me on rare occasions.

I revived her body, but her spirit had gone.

Namaste… To the Father and to the Son and to the Holy Spirit and to my Guardian Angel as well … Namaste… I say it every morning.

"A crook is a crook until proven innocent, as they can't correct themselves from doing what they do."- My words as Trump is a crook... "A gangster, and not even a good one." - Robert DeNiro.

My Old Ass... a charming love story with a twist ... Very cathartic and a profound message that you can't let yourself live in the past ... along with seeing a woman's T-Shirt... "Saved by Grace and Coffee." My two miracles of love today... I'm blessed.

"I am, therefore I think."- A.I. and to be taken seriously...

Checks and Balances... What a concept... Not anymore!!...

Trump is determined to destroy the world... Why? ... WHY?

Our brains think we're in control, but the reality is it's the bigger picture of it all that moves us forward... Where to then?... Anybody's guess... Be present and accounted for in the here and now.

Morning... The beginning of a new day, or to grieve what once was near and dear... A bit of both, I think... IT still hurts.

Some of us are indeed otherworldly... Heavenly bodies...

Earthbound Angels... "Ruth was an angel walking among us." A friend commented once or twice, as she was just that.

What's your Tipping Point? ... "Get busy living or get busy dying."- Shawshank Redemption... City of Angels, too... Two amazing movies that are a Must See... "Are you in despair?" Nicholas Cage asks.

9/28/2024, and Asheville, NC, is in ruins... We shared so many good times there over the years... Mother Nature can be cruel at times... Climate change is real and in crisis... Someone described the flow of water through Asheville as greater than that of Niagara Falls... if you can imagine? ...

"No more Grieving... for ourselves... Because those that we have lost... ARE IN A HEAVENLY PLACE... So, it's for ourselves that we grieve... They're in a Perfect Place surrounded by Love." - My brother's words struck a nerve and a raw one at that, as I let the weight of the Sad Stone I've been carrying go and now realize that no one grieves in heaven, as they're all too busy praising G-D and celebrating life... We must wish them well.

I will honor them all with my Rebirth Day and spring forward from now on... My grief has finally been put to rest... R.I.P. ... Fingers crossed.

What's next, as it's anybody's guess... Unnerving uncertainty.

"The pain of being transformed and rearranged while still alive often feels unbearable… Reexperience the world freshly." *The Book of Awakening* by Mark Nepo.

"Sometimes we're expected to give a Herculean Effort we never thought we'd be capable of."- My conclusion.

"When kindness can save your life, it becomes like a miracle," and "You can't change the past, but the past can change you." White Bird.

Emanuel = G-D with us … Always… Omnipresent and Omnipotent as well… Accept it.

"Think you can or think you can't, either way you're right."- Anonymous

Hurricane Milton is about to destroy much of FL… If you're hiding in a bush outside Mara-logo… "It's time to shelter in place."- Bill Marr

10/10/2024 … I said G-D bless to a total stranger, and she thanked me and said she needed that… and we fist bumped and smiled… Meant to be… A shared moment of Grace… Lovely.

"Are you looking for something… OR … Someone?" - Wicked… and a great pickup line.

10/11/1975- 1st SNL Weekend Update… "The Post Office has decided to issue a Stamp to commemorate Prostitution… It's a 10-cent Stamp, but if you want to lick it, it's a quarter."- And "Live from NY … It's Saturday Night… 50 years ago… Wow!!

"It doesn't get easier; it just gets less hard." … And … "I'm probably the best I've been in a really long time."- The Outrun … One day at a time is the best we can do… A movie about Alcoholism… Made me realize my own addictions.

Birthdays come and Birthdays go, and age is just a number… I believe we are ageless, eternal beings here by the Grace of God.

"I hope you had the time of your life." Happy Birthday, Mr. Kevin… A good but strange friend over the years… He loved Bogie and Ruth very much.

"Sometimes 20/20 hindsight may be too little too late."- Me.

Allow me to state the obvious, and that is that WWIII has in fact begun… The Middle East, Russia, Ukraine, China, Japan, North Korea, and the USA… All about to push each other's buttons just to see what happens … It's gonna get ugly and painful, as we could have prevented it but apparently chose not to… Sorry to be so morose, but I had to speak my mind… I hope I'm wrong… I think we're living in the Dark Ages from now on.

I watched "The Age of Adeline" with Blake Lively and a modern take on living without ever aging… A sort of modern version of The Portrait of Dorian Gray… One of my all-time favorite movies… See the original one if ever you can.

"Exceptionally wonderful."- My time with Ruth.

I think my solitude has been my salvation, allowing me to think and write… I have so much to be grateful for indeed… I've had some very profound rambling conversations with myself, in private… Turns out I'm a good listener.

I amaze myself sometimes when I look at some of my creations over the years… Art@Work Including my writing … "I write… No, you wrong!"- a line from a western years ago.

"Ha-Ha-Ha… Ho-Ho-Ho and a couple of La-Di-Daz… That's how we pass the day away in the merry old land of OZ" … The Wizard of Oz and still my favorite… "1939" and Amazing for the time.

Our health is our greatest wealth and our responsibility. "Make good choices." … Stay strong and in charge, and what I told my brother… Change is not always for the better.

"As human beings, we are resilient beyond anything we can imagine… Seek the truth, and by doing so, we change."- Mark Nepo.

"If you want to predict the future, you shape the future."- Joe Scarborough on MSNBC… Brilliant.

Bernard La Pierre… Governor of the Côte d'Ivoire, Africa, 1870. My mom's great-grandfather… We have a picture and see our Mum in his face.

I'm open to what's next, as 25 years ago, a magic moment did present itself, and it all unfolded with Ruth on 11/22/1999.

"Come in she said I'll give you Shelter from the storm."- Bob Dylan.

Truth be told, I experienced more than I ever imagined I would, and for that I'm grateful… We were very blessed.

Change is indeed inevitable and doesn't necessarily mean for the better… My experience… We must be more careful these days… Evil does exist… Praise G-D and rebuke evil!!

As I exited through the mall parking area, I came upon an MGB-GT with an older gentleman behind the wheel … I had to stop to say hello, and he shared that it was in fact a 1975 and one of only three just like it, with the steering wheel on the right… Mine was a 1974, and the car my father died in… I shared that seeing IT made my day … A meant to be moment for sure… Thank you.

"My life is Unlimited… Sky's the limit !!… I hope you're happy now."- Wicked… A question we need to ask more often.

I went for my eye exam today, and when they told me that I might have to pay for what's not covered by insurance… I asked IF they accept Library Cards, Social Security, or Bingo, and they all cracked up… Still funny after all these years… My Thanksgiving prayer is to simply praise God every day, several times a day, as Thanksgiving should be every day.

To Richard Royce: I'd say thank you, old man, and until we meet again, and fait-vaux-jeus… and Bon-chance… Good work… I'm sure we'll cross paths again and again… Thanks for coming.

"We never stop choosing who we are." … And… "There's always another way."- Moana… Always.

"We have all come from a hard past." … What do you miss most? … To ponder… Love and affection, intimacy and joy… I'm not happy anymore… My Debbie-Downer days I guess… Still.

Compassion and Empathy are everything… It's what love is.

"Always look on the bright side of life."- Monte Python.

I pray that the Lord show me what is truly important.

I remain Hope-Phil and Joy-Phil… "Happiness runs in a circular motion, floating like a little boat upon the sea… Everybody is a part of everything anyway; you can be happy if you let yourself be."- The 1st song Monte taught me 50 years ago in Israel.

Do you have a dream now, and what is it teaching you?

"We don't make great decisions when we think with our genitalia."- My appreciation.

I'm leaving a trail behind of who I was as a person.

"Take the path of least resistance," My financial advisor told me… We love sharing dirty jokes and laughing out loud together… I trust his advice in growing what money I have left.

Both Thanksgiving and Hanukkah should be celebrated each and every day, I think… The celebration of miracles and gratitude…

I just learned that a very large asteroid passed us fairly close… I saw Interstellar, and it was actually like a modern-day version of the movie 2001 years ago, and was very well done.

"Killing time is murder."-Anonymous.

Can I create a new life for myself here in NC, and if not here, then where? … I continue to honor her past.

Happiness doesn't come sitting still… Happiness runs!

"ONE is the loneliest number you'll ever know… TWO can be as bad as one, but the loneliest number is the number 1"- Three Dog Night.

You are approaching a crossroads in your journey… I try my best to make good choices every day.

I picked up a prescription… washed and charged my car… Got a few things at the grocery store… Got a haircut… Watched some Ancient Aliens… Made some Chicken and Rice and peas and appreciated all I've been given … Grace from above, really.

Sometimes, when we least expect it, the universe gives us what we need, and the magic of the moment can happen at any time.

"I want to live again, Lord."- George Bailey… in It's a Wonderful Life… "Let me live again." … "Let me live again."- George prays out loud with great humility… He was given a great gift.

My realization is that I will never find another quite like Ruth, as you only get one true love… She was IT.

Our Bizaaro-World is now The Un-United States of Trumpmerica… Sad but true, as we've lost our way… The new normal ain't normal no more, and may never be again, I fear.

"Life isn't fair, but eventually we will get to The Promised Land." … I pray it's true… We'll see them all again for sure.

We, the people, don't mean the 1%. The wealthy do not understand us or our reality… We now live in The Twilight Zone and The Outer Limits as the craziest people are in charge… Crazy world then… No choice at this point… "We're Doomed."- Ruth used to say on occasion, and she might be right this time.

"Sometimes life grabs you by the short hair and doesn't let go, just to mess with us and remind us who's really in charge."

Today's paradigm shift might be just what we've been hoping for… Let's be open to it and grateful as well.

Is there a question you would ask me? … What? … Ask me then … What a journey life is… But it goes by too quickly… Much too quickly.

"I am so glad that I have been fortunate enough to have my Shirpa (You) with me… all the time."- Sandys' words to me today… I think we're both each other's Shirpa at this point… We both just needed a friend in our lives… Someone to lean on and laugh with as well.

"The world in all its mystery and difficulty cannot be improved upon, but only experienced."- A lesson of Taoism.

I can't help but think the entire world is about to experience a brutal change for the worse… Much worse, maybe… I hope not.

Three years in the making, and it's done. "Very Interesting Perspectives" is going to print… My story is told and will soon be ready to share… My thoughts are exposed for all to see, and I'm happy it's done… Very much a Herculean Effort… and very healing as well… "V.I.P."

"Twas The Farce before Christmas." Trump/Musk … They're letting us know how wild and really crazy they are.

Markers for change… Take action… Do it!!

Stretch - Neck Roll / Shoulder Roll / Arms behind head stretch / Hip twist / Ankle Roll / Back bending / Push-ups off sink… Drink more water and V8 !!… And lose 20 lbs … BP is of concern.

Ruth and I used to walk around a small lake behind our townhouse in Governors Village, and we'd stop at a wooden bridge to say a prayer for someone who'd recently passed…

I went there to make a prayer for her, as it's been three years since she passed… I told her that if she needs to transition to her next plane, that it's okay, and I want her to… Go, then, I said, and we'll reconnect later… A Golden Retriever appeared & gave me kisses so I knew she was there… Ruth had owned a Golden Retriever when we first met, and it was so very meaningful… We called him Samalama-Dingdong, and he loved chasing squirrels.

Aging is not a crime… but it does feel a little like punishment sometimes… I went to a Podiatrist recently because I had a corn on my left pinky toe, and an X-ray revealed that my big toe is 95% arthritis stricken at this point… Not what I'd hoped for, but it is what it is.

"Find your footing one step at a time." Tai Chi walking.

A new year is coming… Let's make it a good one… 2025

"Practicing gratitude and manifesting abundance." A commercial reminds us.

I'm reminded that Thanksgiving, Christmas, and Hanukkah should all be celebrated every day.

I think that if ever I'm offered the chance to do it all again by reincarnating, I might choose not to, for as much joy as we get to savor, there's just too much pain and sadness.

My perpetual weakness is what I once had with Ruth and Sandy, his Eileen… We were both so blessed to have had them in our lives.

Jimmy Carter… He was a good man and a deeply spiritual person as well as a rak-on-tur' … someone who tells stories with skill… A Peanut Farmer who became President… Well done, kind Sir, well done… He was also an artist and a carpenter.

He also won the Nobel Peace Prize and accomplished more after his term as president than any other president, and he is an exemplary human being… A one of a kind… We need more like him… "We can choose to work together for peace."- His words. An angel walking among us … Christ-like even.

"A man of great character and courage."- Biden on Carter.

My awareness as we're about to end this year is that I not only survived, but in fact accomplished what I'd hoped in writing my book, as it took 3 years and is more than I'd ever thought it might be… So with a new year before me, I'm ready to embrace whatever comes next… A new chapter in a yet unwritten new book, maybe … "Loose Ends & Screws…" is that extra chapter in this Revised Edition at this point.

12/31/2024 is both an end followed with a new beginning… 1/1/2025 then… "Happy New You." … Everyday really.

I'm reminded of the Joni Mitchell song where she says that she's "seen her life from both sides now… Round & round & round in the circle game." … Do you think we'll make it to 2050? I asked my brother. It won't be pretty if we do.

"Don't forget to poop before midnight… You don't want to carry the same shit from last year into 2025," My sister Nic told me. "But who would we be without our shit?" - To ponder, I told her.

"We are blessed in this time, this place to be human beings alive in rare ways that we often take for granted… So, what will you do today… How will you carry yourself and what will you do with your hands?" - *The Book of Awakening* by Mark Nepo.

"You are precious, rare, and awake."- Today's lesson.

"I think a change would do you good."- Sheryl Crow.

I recently shared with my brother Marc, who is looking into moving in with my brother Sandy … A Herculean gesture and effort for them both… It's what family does Sandy declared.

"Oh, what a beautiful morning, oh what a beautiful day."- An old song I'm remembering.

"Life is in session."- Anthony Hopkins shared 49 years of sobriety before his 87th birthday … I love it… To life then.

I'm walking like an old man as my arthritic left foot is not doing well… Looking for options, and it doesn't look like I'll need surgery… Huge relief!!

We're not meant to understand it all, but asked to accept it as it unfolds one day at a time… Is what it is… "How did we get here, and where are we going?"

When my book arrived… "Wow, that is so beautiful… I'm sure you feel extremely gratified with your accomplishment… Fucking great."- An old friend commented … 3 years in the making and my Herculean Effort…

"Now it's time to plan a sequel," May Su told me.

We are all unique and yet the same.

"Makin' Progress."- Ruth used to say … Life is an uphill battle…

Fight the good fight. "Attack your day."- Andy Boy Schaefer

"We do what we must do and we do it well."- Anonymous

Make it a good day… My life included Ruth for 22 years, and it felt much longer, as we enjoyed so much… So very much.

At 71, I'm looking back on it all, remembering as much as I can, as it won't ever be the same without them… The Circle of Life… I've experienced the deer and the dog and the butterfly and the bluebird and blue jay as well… and each with my awareness and appreciation, and so significant in the moment.

After my final corrections, I printed 13 copies of my book to give away… I'm now ready to move on without them… as I must at this point…

What and who comes next is in G-D's hands, and I must trust in The Lord to guide me to my next adventure.

"Say what you mean and mean what you say… and know that you can withstand the experience of conflict that living requires."

I'm in need of an emotional rescue and some real affection at this point… Tenderness even… Love maybe.

"It looks like Hiroshima."- Jay Leno in regards to CA fires.

"How we decide to rise from the ashes … If I have, you have, and if you have, I have."- An old black CA man shared with us all.

"A beacon of freedom."- Joe Biden … He will be greatly missed… "We must not be bullied into sacrificing our future." … Let's remember his words… "May G-D protect the truth." … This Romper-Room Administration will destroy the world… He's the devil in drag… No doubt… I pray for his removal.

Let me be the 1st to boo our new administration … As nothing good can come of it… We're fucked, as now billionaires will have their way while the rest of us watch in disbelief!!

Levels of solitude are surging while loneliness is flat… The nightly news reported not long ago.

Ruth got me a bar of soap from Nashville, TN, once, wrapped in music with "I walk the line" as a quote from Johnny Cash… So poignant and profound as she walked The Line to the end… My tears of joy hide my tears of sadness, and vice versa.

The Next Room… One woman is terrified of dying while another is about to end her life… Cancer and Chemo-Brain sucks, she shared… She could no longer concentrate and simply longed for peace… Some of us suffer better than others… They got to accompany each other, and her death made them closer… The snow is falling on the living and the dead… The End… A powerful performance and message as well.

1/18/2025 … Aware that the #18 = Life and feeling blessed and grateful for it all… From beginning to end, we have been greatly blessed… The significance of bridges in my life is profound.

A wooden bridge near where we used to live always reminded me of what our papa wanted to build across our pond… We used to stop to make a prayer for someone who'd recently passed… A very colorful version was offered up shortly after Ruth's passing, and how she now sees it… Yet another version of a bridge on my parents' wedding anniversary to let me know they hear me... and today I realized that I reside at The Bridges of Chapel Hill... Synchronicity for sure.

I think these next 4 years or more will be known as "The Darker Ages." ... Maybe The Darkest Ages... Sad but true.

1/20/2025 ... Let The Shit-Show begin ... Trump should borrow Steve Martin's Arrow in his head prop for his speech ... One wild and crazy guy... The beginning of The End... G-D help us... It's a sad day for the entire world.

Trump lost any and all possible benefit of the doubt 34 consecutive convictions ago ... The man's a criminal... Period... He's a demented old circus monkey... Elect a Clown, expect a Circus... Beyond belief, pocketing billions for himself.

Elon Musk salutes using a Hitler-style wave... Looks like our new Commander-in-Chief has shown inexcusable and unpardonable behavior in his 1st 24 hours ... OMG... PRAY.

I created my Zen Garden homage to all we shared, and I feel her continued presence and gratitude for all we did together ... It went by too quickly, but was great while it lasted... 1/23/2025 and 3rd anniversary of her passing... "Once in a lifetime, never again."- A Japanese saying, and so poignant.

To stay or to move? ... To ponder... Where to then? ... Where to?

I'm as strong as I needed to be ... I felt her presence with me on the 23rd and know she's alive and well in the next experience we will all eventually get to see.

My realization is that I don't know how you deal with your stuff and you don't know how I deal with my stuff... and yet we all just do our best and deal with it... My words to Mark and Em as a sort of Olive Branch, I think, maybe.

My story is not an easy read, but no one's life is, I think... Fast and Pray... Pray and Fast.

Trump 2.0 = 1 step forward and 2 or 3 steps back... Maybe more?... Many more.... America's new Liar-in-Chief... President Doom and V.P. Gloom from now on.

"Your heart is like a miraculous balloon, its lightness comes from staying full ... Meeting the days with one's heart prevents collapse."- The

Book of Awakening by Mark Nepo … Today's message I meant to send to my brother Marc, but instead sent to my accountant, who I was scheduled to see later that day… He appreciated it, and our meeting resulted in a $1500 Tax Refund… Sweet!

Then, while at the checkout at the grocery store, I frequent, a black woman behind me got my attention and I told her to go ahead of me … She was thankful and shared her challenges with Arthritis … I shared Collagen Peptides as something that might help, and her joy was brilliant… "Happy New Year," she said.

"You know it's not the same as it was, as it was… As it was." Harry Styles … I love his message and meaningful truth.

It's the year of the snake, and time to shed our skin and any negativity we have. "It's going to be a great day." … "Still Crazy after all these years."- Paul Simon … Still crazy.

We risk being alone until the glow of life presents itself.

"Please take care of yourself and each other."- Lester Holt.

He recently retired from the Nightly News and will be missed.

Ruth could speak volumes without saying a word… A look was all it took… "Hello Stranger." … Her words every now and then.

Some dance their way into Heaven like David Bowie, and others skate into Heaven like we just witnessed, and most just find themselves there one day… Life after death is bigger and better than we ever expected.

Wishful thinking vs. Foolish thinking vs. Thinking out loud… which would you choose?… All 3 at times, maybe.

To see new things is to see things anew… The picture of the Manteo boardwalk where we'd visited during our last road trip was my miracle of love once, as I was waiting for my car to be serviced… It spoke to me and let me know she was near… Always near, just out of reach… She's happy, and I'm glad for her.

Forever and Eternal, as Ruth shared with the Chinese wind chime she'd left for me to find on top of our fridge… Got it.

Trump and Musk prove that 2 heads are not better than one. Two heartless people in the wrong place at the wrong time. The worst of the worst, and heartless as the new Pope showed his dismay with meeting Vance… "Next" was his immediate thought.

I had a powerful dream of both Mum and Nic being in bed together, sharing a moment filled with joy and happiness… Her smiling face was all a glow.

69 years of life experience and all the wisdom and enlightenment you've gathered along the way should make another day easier, I hope… You're still here and still standing, so bring it on, as they say, for a while longer… Love you much… My words to Sandy on his birthday.

The fact of the matter is that if I had it all to do over again, I wouldn't change a thing… Sandy and I both agreed.

2/9/2025 and Super Bowl Sunday… "All progress has a starting point," One player shared.

One day at a time, one step at a time… Be blessed… Feel blessed… Go forth and bless others.

Today is yesterday's tomorrow… and time is the unreal reflection of eternity… "The unreal reflection of eternity."- Anonymous, and so true.

Be here now… Here is where we want to be… An interesting movie with Tom Hanks filmed in one room… See it if you can. He's such a great actor and will forever be our Forrest Gump.

Papa told us about Geographically Undesirable… but there's also Emotional and Intellectual undesirability."- My words to my brother and his Kyra… We live with the choices we make.

Good Morning, Brother. finished your Book last night… It made me appreciate your pain, both old and recent… And the fact that you're still standing… Thanks for sharing and still being there for all of us… Enjoy the weekend.

After Trump's first month, I have to wonder if the world can survive four years? I don't think we will frankly… He actually wants to be king for the rest of his life… and rule the world… Really?

"A severe, untreatable personality disorder and malignant narcissism, and he also suffers from cognitive decline." His niece commented as being a clinical Psychiatrist herself. "Trump lives in a disinformation bubble."- Zelenskyy and well stated as their meeting at the White House was an insult to the world, and demo-crazy for all to see… Demo-Crazy.

Feels like we're becoming the USA-R… Doz-Ve-Dania Rouskie … Seriously. "An Existential Crisis."- MSNBC announced, stating the obvious out loud for us to digest.

"Every day may not be good, but there is some good in every day."-Anonymous.

What makes a house a home?… Making good choices.

The curve is upward … The learning curve.

Here's a really bad joke… Trump and all his cabinet choices… especially the numb-nut with the chainsaw… A truly corrupt conspiracy to control our world.

I had an awareness of separation and distancing today as no one connected to my messages, and I realize that it's okay, and it's time for me to move on without them.

"Realize that there are no wrong turns, only unexpected paths… Don't ya know… for sure, hey… Miracles are everywhere if you're open to it."-Today's lesson and I saw I'm Still Here and can relate to the title… It was very good… Thanks for grabbing my attention from the Box Office window as you made me smile… My words to Lauri … "Thank you for being a friend." I told her.

I connected with three friends and both of my brothers via text and bought some stamps, then mailed a couple of bills… Bought a roasted chicken for $5.00, which will make 3 or 4 meals … Washed my sheets and vacuumed and did some recycling as well… Got gas and connected with a gentleman who was gassing up his Porsche… We both shared a moment of appreciation of finer Automobiles… I'm enjoying a salad with a glass of wine, appreciating how the world has gone mad after just one month of Trump's 2.0 … I hope you had a good day.

On 2/24/2025, the next American Revolution has begun to take shape with an upside-down flag in Yosemite Park.

"A billionaire runs amok." … Our new reality and paradigm shift… Let's call his bluff is all I can say… Looks like China is doing just that… Trump Tariffs prove he doesn't get it… He's earned the nickname "TACO" as Trump Always Chickens Out… He hates the name and claims he's negotiating… Such BS!

My health has taken a downturn with concerns about my prostate … 95% Arthritis in my left foot and lower back issues as well … Not good, and Dr. Apts. in April and May will reveal what's what.

I live one day at a time and stay connected to a handful of friends, as it's all I can do to stay sane these days simply.

Monty's birthday, and we can only hope that our shared life together exceeded their expectations… It was good while it lasted, and they knew it… Barooch Ha Shem.

Appreciate that my PTSD and my book V.I.P. is my story of healing… Post Traumatic Stress Disorder… It's real… Sad as well as I can cry at any time… and still shed tears almost daily.

The Oval Office Debacle… Irreparable damage… Stupid is as stupid does. "Kabuki Theater." … The world is watching… Hard to watch as they act like they know what they're doing… They don't, and can't bully their way out either… A real Shit-Show.

A new day to share with__ ?… IDK… I'm at a loss and can only keep praying on it… Lord knows I need a hug from someone.

Shortly after Papa passed, Sandy experienced walking with him through the woods, until they came to a fork… "This is where we part," he said, "but we'll see each other again one day."- Papa's reminder to us all on this day, some 48 years later… 3/5/1977 … Barooch Ha Shem… Amen and Amen… Anyway, we'll see them all again one day… No doubt… "Come tous jour."- Our Mum used to say … She's alive and well, as are they all.

Appreciate for a brief moment what our relatives survived… IT should give us both pause and strength to stand tall and keep on keeping on one day at a time… We must grab our bootstraps and pull ourselves up each and every day.

"We'll figure it out," Ruth used to say on occasion.

The New World Disorder is that we're the USA-R and Trump is in bed with Putin… KGB maybe even… A Rouskie-Chrooye… (A Russian Prick) … Two demented leaders going nowhere.

3/6/2025 "STOP Crying!" … My brother told me… What can I say except that he makes me laugh, smile, and cry as well. I'm still recovering from PTSD and bear the open wound that may never fully heal.

Seak and ye shall find… Be your best self… You got this…

Welcome to my world, and my renaissance… This is me… We're not meant to understand… We're simply asked to come along for the ride… The ride of your life… Enjoy it IF possible.

"The world has fallen off its Axis."- my brother's words… Wow.

I went for ice cream and felt her with me… It was Date-like.

"Is what it is and was what it was." Time to move on, time to get going… "I have no regrets, neither should you."- A great quote from Mission Impossible… I told my brother to cry… It's healing… He should let himself cry more often than he does.

Is less really more?… Waiting, Trusting, and Hoping are intricately connected… We have been greatly blessed.

Allow yourself to be carried by the spirit we can't see… Have faith and hold God's hand… He'll never let go… PRAY on it.

I'm grateful for my beginning and my end, and everything in between… My awareness every morning as I give thanks.

PTSD and why I wrote V.I.P. Very Interesting Perspectives… My book and my effort to move beyond it… To make sense of it all and to stay alive… I reside in my once-upon-a-time life… Sad but true… Hard to let go… Impossible really… I can't.

My book is my timeline from beginning to end… and my effort to begin again.

We honored our parents' wedding anniversary today, 71 years ago, as had they not wed, none of us would have come along for the ride… I was there, as mum chose to keep this one… Lucky me and lucky us, as they were meant to be… True love was their story… They shared a picture of a bridge with me last year as a miracle of love, letting us know they're alive and well in heaven above, and look at what they indeed influenced. "Family… God's greatest creation."- Yitzhak, our cousin who endured 4 or 5 wars in his lifetime… An amazing person with so much love.

"Would you hide me … a Jewish woman asked her friend, IF it were to ever come to that?" Oct.8 and a movie about the Hamas attack… Brutally shocking, as the problem is much bigger than we'd thought… Antisemitism is a much bigger problem today than any of us realizes… There seems to be a need to hate… Why?

"Cultivate a spirit of humility." … Difficulties either break us or they break us wide open… When we look at another person, we must say: "I could be that person… That person could be me." … Empathy and compassion are always necessary.

Current Events have taken a turn for the worse, and I'm losing any sense of optimism about it… Doom and Gloom, then I guess… I've fallen down the doomscrolling rabbit hole towards catastrophizing… A new word

I just learned… Might be the case for a lot of folks these days… Catastrophizing :(

"Ripples of our memories are always with us … Don't take yourself too seriously… Being takes time."- *The Book of Awakening* by Mark Nepo

The Kingdom, The Power and The Glory forever and ever…

Everything is possible… "This is the day the Lord has made… Let's be glad and rejoice in it."- Robert Schuller

There's inescapable pain in living one's life… Today is a holy day, let's treat it as such… It's always darkest before the dawn.

My NY Trip was my demonstration of commitment to family… We always laugh till it hurts when we're together… Such fun.

First of all, … It's AAALTACKACKOR… Not Al Tacocker… Too funny, as I tried to make it a person named Al, but Sandy didn't get it, and felt he had to correct my spelling… It means Old Turd.

"These are strange times."- Rachel Maddow … Understatement for the day… She's great at what she does and shares so many insights into the madness we're witnessing right now.

"Live for the present."- May Su.

Trump Times… Our Commander of Mischief is proving himself to be the Epitome of Stupidity… and IF aliens from above landed tomorrow, he'd probably order them to Guantanamo Bay… Dumb Fuck… The Trump Administration is an abomination!!

I know happiness is not a continuous state, but it would be nice to experience it again one day… Soon maybe? … IDK.

Life demands that we endure hardship, as Christ endured by example… He was 33 when it ended the way it did… On the cross.

On 3/24/2025, I was inspired to check into the idea of moving… A 55+ Community named Inspire… Brand new and so much to offer… Then Megan appeared, and our shared appreciation was instantaneous… "What apartment are you in?" I asked. "The one next to yours," she answered and smiled." :)… Hmmm?

My miracles/demonstration today included getting a State Tax Refund of $395.00 along with a total security deposit of only $325.00 plus a 2 Months Free Rent option offered as well… I am blessed, inspired maybe even?… To move or not to move?

"The problem with our current administration is that they're all idiots."- Liz Chaney … She, like so many, is shaking her head in disbelief at what we're seeing unfold… It's shocking!

My current location served its purpose as my oasis, and that ultimately allowed me to both heal and write my book … Now it's time for me to step forward with faith and believe that it's meant to be … My Herculean Effort with moving or staying put for another year? … I'm praying on it… I live within my means.

I was able to walk today, for the first time in two months… I'm so very grateful… Our health is our greatest wealth… I need to walk more often.

I'm having 2nd thoughts and thinking out loud…

Yearly rent increases might be too much to bear. … Uncertainty about Social Security and the economy is to be considered as it's anybody's guess where we're in fact going from here on… The world is spinning out of control these days with too much pain being felt in too many places… WHY? … IDK.

Something to be said for keeping a low profile and following the path of least resistance… Who am I trying to impress? … Cash Flow is of concern… The world is crazy… Uncertainty is everywhere today… So, I'm doing my Homework and pushed my move to June 2026 IF I move at all… Something didn't feel right.

"The day I die will be like any other day, only shorter."- Bill Murray … We spend our entire life trying to figure things out… Time to think outside The Box… He had a Great Dane named Apollo, and he was just so beautiful… A Friend was the movie… See it.

"Courage is Contagious."- Kamala Harris reminds us.

"The biggest lie Trump has ever told is that he cares about you… He does not and only cares about himself and his billionaire friends."- House Dem Leader Hakeem Jeffries … Clear as day.

America is speaking up… The world is watching… G-d is as well.

My brother and I still carry our sadness with us. "That's just the way it is, some things will never change."- Bruce Hornsby.

As the markets adjust, the world is shocked and nervous as Trump plays golf… An unbelievable response, as protests are now bigger and going global… A Global Recession is what's expected, and he's only added to it while enriching himself.

Trump Retribution = Demo-Crazy !!… Can he make any worse decisions? … Apparently, he can, as he now wants to be Pope… Talk about Artificial-Intelligence… "Artificial," and only illustrates his lack of intelligence… He's clueless… Stupid even.

The only person judging you is you … My message to my brother.

The Red Roof Inn in Winchester, VA, is holy ground for me as I feel Ruth, Bogie, and my mum there with me… Amazing Grace… We're blessed and have always been blessed and will always be blessed… Wisdom, Hope, Enlightenment, Truth, Love, and Miracles of Love… My journey north continues tomorrow. Croton-on-Hudson, NY, is beautiful… My Sister is blessed to live there.

My miracle of love on Saturday night after Passover was as we arrived at Sandy's apartment around midnight … He'd lit 3 candles before leaving with one for his Lenie… a 2nd for our Mum … and a 3rd for Ruth … The one for her was still lit and burning bright when we walked in, and Sandy shared its profound significance and her presence… Ruth was celebrating with us… Passover 2025 :)…

"I don't have good days anymore," Our Marc shared with us.

"Never just walk by a bathroom… and never let a hard-on go to waste… and never assume that it was just a fart. "- Jack Nicholson … Too funny.

"We have to get our hearts to feel again."- Pope Francis

As I was checking out near customer service, a Tibetan monk appeared in full costume, and appeared uncertain of his mission to get assistance … As I left, I paused to bow and honor his presence… His smile said it all, as we both knew whose in charge.

I woke up recently thinking Sugarloaf, NY, might be an option I should consider… Hmm?… I worked there many years ago.

On 4/22, I'm forwarding chapters of my book to Paula Cruz … Let's see what happens? … She's got a beautiful face, great eyes, and a Mona Lisa smile… "Come a little bit closer." Harvest

Moon by Neil Young? … Meant to be? … No, it is not apparently… Oh well, I tried… She, not so much.

Economic Armageddon and a new term for what's coming… 100 days down and … only 1,360 to go … Not possible or feasible … Just stating the obvious.

"Life is what happens in between making plans."- John Lennon.

Our Papa is in heaven… and a profound awareness and appreciation as well… Our Father in Heaven.

As in all her doings, Ruth always strived to leave it better than it was… and so she did with me as well… Better than before… "Great to have that as your legacy for time on earth," Glenn pointed out.

Do you want this? … What am I willing to sacrifice? … Weigh your options… We must be resolute.

"Tariffs… The biggest self-inflicted wound ever to the American Brand."- CNN 4/27/2025 … He's a buffoon !!…

After his 1st 100 days in office, Trump proves to the world that he thinks he now rules, that indeed he's worth his weight in cow manure… AKA "BS".

Reclaim your right to thrive…

At 2:22 am on 5/3, I was awakened and reminded of mum's birthday, along with my anniversary this day… To life and to love… Forever and Eternal… It's all in G-d's hands… We are each other's miracle of love.

"The thing put to rest becomes the fertilizer for the life about to form."- *The Book of Awakening* by Mark Nepo.

Another Self-Inflicted Moment of Stupidity… Trump as Pope.

On 5/5/2025, I got my FICO credit score, and Ruth would be both pleased and pleasantly surprised, I think… 800 is Exceptional… She sometimes doubted my ability to manage money… I feel her smiling and laughing with me today.

If we look close enough, we can sometimes see the essence of the person, or animal, or a moment of nature … We witness the soul and embrace it… Grace… Amazing !!… Simply Amazing.

"Don't let your hopes be stolen."- Pope Francis.

Ruth came recently as a fat and happy rabbit… We shared a memory of New Orleans and some matzah ball soup we experienced there, along with Mardi Gras… 10 minutes later, she was gone … My miracle of love… She stayed for 10 minutes.

We'd gone to New Orleans for a medical conference during Mardi Gras… Ruth asked me to make a reservation in a restaurant in her hotel, and I waited too long… Nothing was available, and as we walked through the crowd, I could sense her disappointment … Suddenly, 2 seats at the bar opened up, and I grabbed them… She was outside and wondered where I was… Upon venturing back inside, she found me at the bar and said, "Look at you." … So happy and grateful… It was her joy that she reminded me of, as the rabbit symbolized both luck and joy as well.

5/9/2025, and all of a sudden, you're 65… OMG… It all went by so quickly … We are all stronger than we think we are, and best affirmation ever … Enjoy your day and the chocolates I gave you… Happy birthday, Nic… I've known her all her life.

Mother's Day reminds us of how blessed we were to have had them in our lives… They made it look easy even when it wasn't, and they made us who we are today… Thanks Mum, for everything… Everything !!… Love ya.

5/14/2025, and Ruth came to me in a dream and stood in front of me in a winter coat, and both her smile and red hair stood out as she expressed not feeling well… Not sure how to interpret it, but her presence was strong and profound … IT was her.

"Is fate ever exactly how we expect it to be?" … Chaos shows us the way… My two cents.

"86-47"- James Comey, and well said by stating the obvious.

Robert Dinero and Bruce Springsteen speak up as well… Neil Young too … Bono from U2 shared that there's only one Boss in America … Trump is truly hated by so many at this point.

Onward Christian Soldier… Go in search of some significance… My words to my brother… Find your Joi de vie… It's like a game of lost and found… She's out there, looking for the same thing.

"God's illumination decimates any darkness."

5/23/2025 and 2nd anniversary of Mum's passing… Memorial Day weekend with Chapter 7 added to my book as a Revised Edition with new Final Thoughts… Bills paid and Credit Card under control with $12k in checking… "Good Job, Mr. Schaefer," I feel her contentment… "The flame of life is eternal."

Looking into Investment Strategies and planning a Road Trip… Where to then? … IDK… I still feel paralyzed at times… Broken… Not sure why?

It's official… This country is now being run by The Cluster-Fuck Administration… Elect a Clown, expect a Circus.

Are you familiar with the term "Bajibaz"? … As in the current administration scares The Bajibaz out of me.

You made me chuckle yesterday when I told you that we're in that window of when it might end, and you said that you're standing by the open door… Sandy is too funny sometimes.

"The two most important days in your life are the day you were born and the day you find out why."- Mark Twain … Profound.

Home Instead… A Nurse coming to you as an option… Good to know… I'm thinking ahead… I wonder how many years I have left?

Mission Impossible and a Digital Covert Entity… Closer to reality than you think… Tom Cruise was amazing.

"If you have heart, you have hope, and you have heart in you." and "Every life is a universe all its own."- The Life of Chuck by Stephen King … A Masterpiece and a Must See… Magical!

"The waiting is the hardest part."- Tom Petty … I saw him in concert once in Saratoga, NY, with Monte… Bob Dylan, too.

Eating together, sleeping together, along with peeing and pooping and showering, is what it comes down to… Good conversation is also much needed, along with prayer.

I think Trump might be a vampire asking us all to give blood.

"The Trump Library… It will be about the same size as a two-person outhouse and will contain inappropriate reading materials… and now with a 747 parked next to it."- My joke.

"Life is beautiful, Life is GOOD, and Life is never ending… Enjoy every moment," May Sue reminded me.

"Grief is not an emotion—it's an unravelling… A space where something once lived but is now gone… It carves through you, leaving a hollow ache where love once resided."- Jim Carrey "Honor your grief, for it is sacred… It is a testament to the depth of your heart."

"And there lies the testimony to the depth of the love you shared."- Sandy's loving conclusion to my stories… Thank you, kind sir… He's a wise old soul who knows the pain of loss all too well… It cuts like a knife, bleeding through our memories. I think my tears of joy and sadness have become one & the same, as it's hard to tell what triggers them these days… IDK any more. 6/3/2025 Our little brother's 62nd birthday… Congratulations, you made it and are now officially Old… as am I and

Sandy and your sister … We're all old at this point, but we're still here and still standing and doing it one day at a time… It's all any of us can do… So, keep on keeping on and appreciate what you can when you can… We are all love and all connected… Happy Birthday… He was so appreciative as I included a handful of choice pictures to remind him of our good times together. XOXO

I think we're all in search of some significance in our lives… Something real with someone real… Maybe it's too much to ask for or expect? … I feel broken at this point, trying my best to imagine some new reality if possible… I'm not sure it is… We shared too many great moments together not to miss them all… It's not possible… It can't be done… IT Sucks being left behind without them… The Silence is indeed Deafening… Their voices are no more… and so I've tried to remember as much as I could.

Go then, in search of some significance… is my best advice…

Good luck… and may G-D Bless… The Lord is our shepherd, and Schaefer in German means shepherd… Coincidence? I think not.

It really began for me with her words "Come & Go with me" in a classified ad she'd written to avoid paying an entrance fee to a Costume party… She wrapped some Christmas lights around herself & wore a green sweater to become a Christmas Tree. :)… Beautifully simple and simply beautiful… "Thank you, Ruth."

"Me… Myself… and I" … All 3 of Me…

Parents

www.ingramcontent.com/pod-product-compliance
Lightning Source LLC
Chambersburg PA
CBHW071754120626
46550CB00002B/782